TECHNOLOGY OF THE

F1

CAR

TECHNOLOGY OF THE

F1
CAR

Nigel Macknight

HAZLETON PUBLISHING

publisher
RICHARD POULTER

production manager
STEVEN PALMER

managing editor
ROBERT YARHAM

art editor
STEVE SMALL

sales promotion
ANNALISA ZANELLA

**marketing and
new media manager**
NICK POULTER

photography by
BRYN WILLIAMS/crash.net

with additional contributions by

LAT PHOTOGRAPHIC
KEVIN CHEVIS
AP RACING
COSWORTH RACING
FERRARI
FLUENT EUROPE
HEXCEL COMPOSITES
HONDA
ILMOR ENGINEERING
ORANGE ARROWS F1
PTC
SPARCO
TOYOTA MOTORSPORT

First published in 2002

ISBN 1-874557-68-3

Acknowledgements

For their co-operation in the research for this book, many thanks to: Jonathan Tubb of Advanced Fuel Systems; Steve Bryan of AP Racing; Nick Hayes of Cosworth Racing; Rob Williamson of Dynamic Suspensions; Robin Butler of Cranfield Impact Centre; Claudio Berro of Ferrari; Dr Chris Humphris and Debbi Marlow of Fluent Europe; Paula Rissanen of Ilmor Engineering; Paul Gately and Tim Harrison of PTC; Simona Signorotto of Sparco; Paul Pomfret of Xtrac.

Printed in Italy by Amadeus Industria Poligrafica Europea SpA

Hazleton Publishing Ltd is a member of Profile Media Group Plc

distributors

UNITED KINGDOM	NORTH AMERICA	REST OF THE WORLD
Haynes Publishing Plc	Motorbooks International	Menoshire Ltd
Sparkford	PO Box 1	Unit 13
Near Yeovil	729 Prospect Avenue	21 Wadsworth Road
Somerset BA22 7JJ	Osceola	Perivale
Telephone: 01963 442030	Wisconsin 54020, USA	Middlesex UB6 7LQ
Fax: 01963 440001	Telephone: (1) 715 294 3345	Telephone: 020 8566 7344
	Fax: (1) 715 294 4448	Fax: 020 8991 2439

CONTENTS

DEFINING THE CONCEPT

A FORMULA 1 racing car is a lean and highly-bred machine. At rest, it looks somewhat ungainly, although beauty is in the eye of the beholder. In motion, in its true element, it is transformed. The car's pace and agility belie its appearance. The Laws of Physics appear not to apply to it. It moves in a way that seems other-worldly. Conventional notions of speed and distance, inertia and articulation evaporate. The car exists in a world apart.

The purpose of this book is to illuminate the process by which a Formula 1 car is conceived, created and driven — placing particular emphasis on racetrack action to illustrate the key principles.

All of the rules governing the design and manufacture of Formula 1 cars are promulgated by the Fédération Internationale de l'Automobile (FIA), headquartered in Paris. Central to these regulations is the requirement that teams must produce their own cars: they cannot purchase proprietary chassis in the way that teams do in almost every other class of motor sport. Despite this fact, if Formula 1 cars raced without paintwork or logos, it would be difficult for the average racegoer to distinguish one car from another. This is because the regulations are so restrictive that there is no opportunity for a bold leap in design philosophy. There are rules governing the overall length of the cars, their width and height, the dimensions of their aerodynamic appendages and dozens of other parameters. These dimensions are checked against templates mounted in strategic positions on the car by FIA scrutineers.

This apparent uniformity is misleading. In reality, the cars bristle with innovative details — as this book will show.

THE PROCESS of designing a Formula 1 car tends to be evolutionary rather than revolutionary, year on year. There is a strong tendency to make an existing concept better rather than discard it totally and start over. In fact, a certain percentage of components is often carried over from the previous year's car in the interests of reliability — particularly those components that have no direct impact on lap times, such as elements of the fuel system. Teams often test components for next year's car during the preceding season, bolting them to the car that is about to be superseded.

In days past, the skills of an exceptional driver could make up for the deficiencies of an improperly designed car, but that is no longer the case. The plain fact is, in Formula 1 today, the chief designer is as valuable to a team as its number one driver and, as a consequence, the top designers command huge salaries — often exceeding those of many drivers. For example, Gustav Brunner *(above)* was reputedly paid in the region of $4 million to leave Minardi (which was paying him $1 million per year) and join Toyota.

In sharp contrast to earlier eras, when individual designers were credited with designing entire cars almost single-handedly, modern Formula 1 cars are designed by a large team of designers, due to the sheer complexity of the design process. The top teams employ 30–35 design personnel — many of whom are tasked with 'detailing' specific aspects of the design, such as the transmission, the front and rear suspension, and so forth. In addition, the top teams typically employ a further 20 personnel in research and development.

THE WHOLE process of designing and building a Formula 1 car takes around six months. Patrick Head, Technical Director of the Williams team, has characterised the process as 'very long and tortuous', and added, 'You've got to have a lot of patience and it's bloody hard work!'

Designing a Formula 1 car requires painstaking scrutiny of the FIA's 'Yellow Book' — the book of regulations — and a determined effort to gain every possible advantage within the limited scope of the rules. Increasingly in Formula 1, the written regulations are 'fleshed out' by clarifications from the FIA in response to specific proposals from car designers: teams are obliged to ask when they wish to stray into a grey area. The FIA takes the view that governing in this manner is the only realistic way, because designers will always find a route around published rules.

There are four major phases in the design of a Formula 1 car: conceptual scheming, preliminary scheming, final scheming and detailing. Although some scheming is done with pencil and paper on a drawing board, the vast majority of design activities are computer-based. Draughtsmanship has been supplanted by 'modelling', in which representations of components are generated digitally and displayed on-screen in 3D. This is computer-aided design (CAD), and it allows designers to modify their designs quickly and relatively easily, without having to redraw components every time a change is made.

Once created, a 'model' can be manipulated at will. For example, the designer can 'rotate' a component, allowing it to be viewed from any angle, or he can 'slice' the component at any point along its length, allowing it to be viewed in cross-section. He can also check that there will be adequate clearance between components before they are manufactured and installed in the car. Furthermore, '3D modelling' allows the weight, and weight distribution, of any component to be automatically calculated at any stage in the design process.

When a CAD system is linked to a group of machine tools by a process called computer numerical control (CNC), the capability is extended to become computer-aided manufacture (CAM). In a CAD/CAM environment — sometimes called computer-aided engineering (CAE) — components that have been modelled on-screen can be partially or wholly manufactured with minimal human intervention, saving precious time.

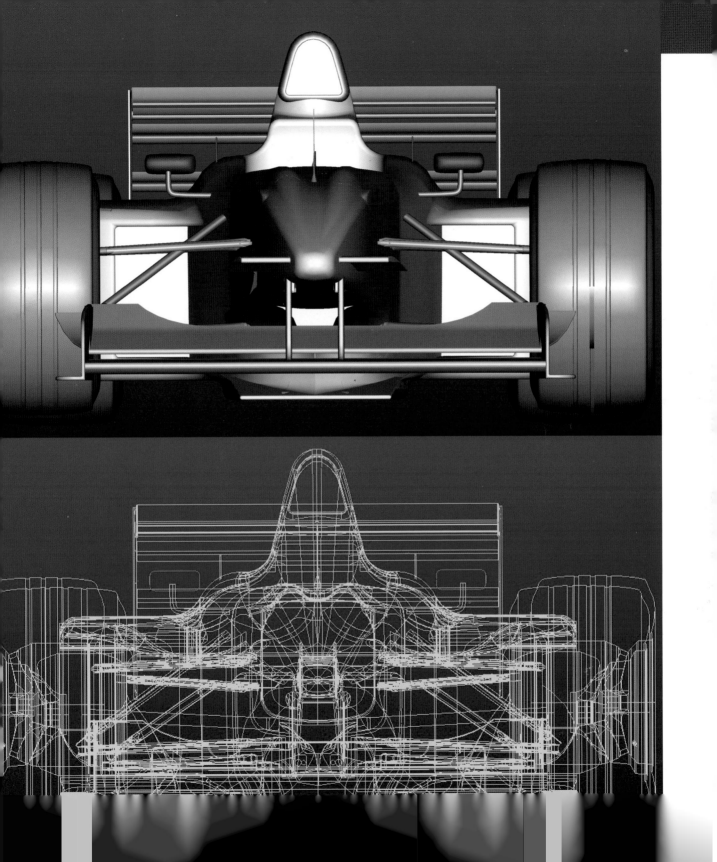

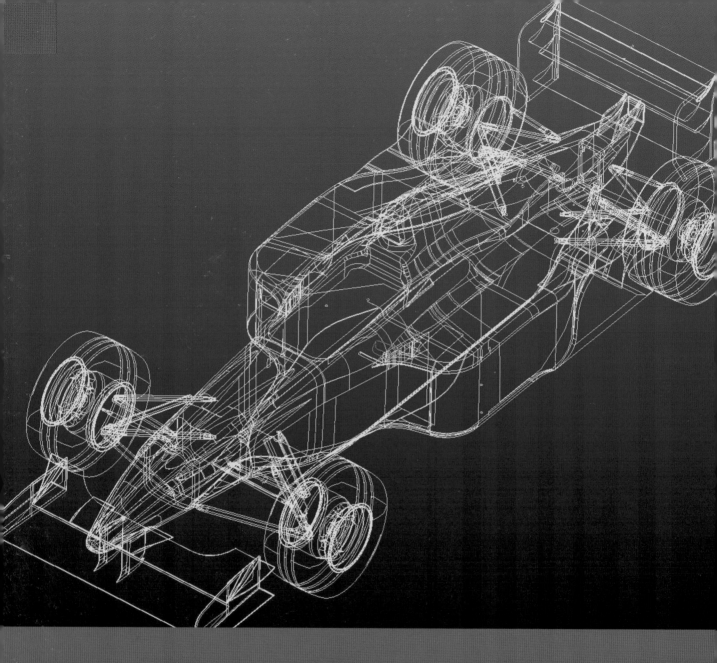

Another way this capability speeds the design/build process is with 'rapid prototyping'. In this relatively new sphere of engineering, a machine similar to an inkjet printer, linked to the CAD system, builds up layers of wax to produce physical representations of components that have been designed on-screen. The machine can be left to run overnight, allowing designers the following morning to view and physically handle a component (or, rather, a near-identical approximation of it) before committing to the costly and time-consuming process of manufacturing it in metal. Wax representations of components produced in this way can even be used to cast actual components, such as gearbox casings.

Rather than purchasing the hardware and software needed to undertake CAD, which is extremely expensive, most teams enter into commercial agreements with hardware manufacturers and software developers, whereby the CAD equipment and peripherals are supplied free of charge as a form of sponsorship. For example, Jaguar's CAD hardware is supplied by Hewlett Packard, while Ferrari's CAD software (Pro/ENGI-NEER) comes from PTC.

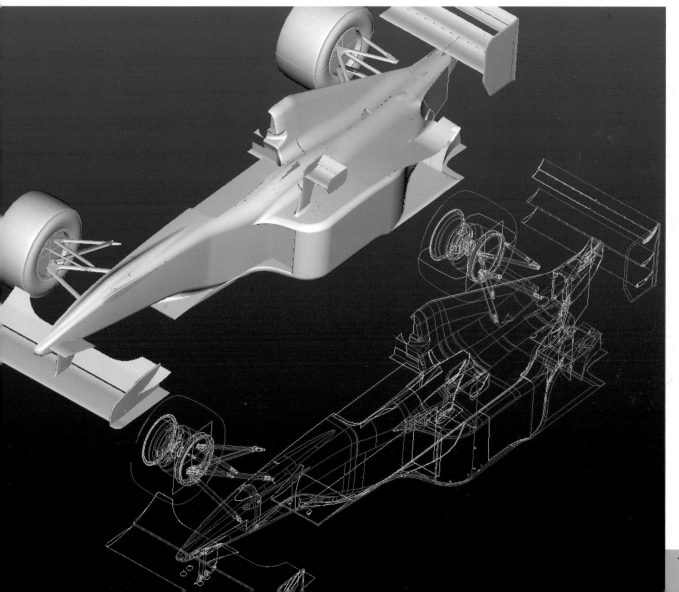

THERE IS little or no scope to produce an innovative vehicle layout in Formula 1, because the regulations effectively define the order in which the key elements of the car are disposed, front to rear. Starting at the front, the driver's feet must be a mandatory distance behind the front axle line, for safety reasons. Working back from that, the fuel must be stored entirely behind the driver, again for safety reasons. The engine and gearbox will inevitably be located behind the fuel, so the geometry of front axle/driver/fuel/engine/gearbox is effectively dictated.

Even if the regulations were freer, the dimensions of some elements of the car cannot be significantly altered, no matter how talented the designer — most notably the dimensions of the cockpit, which must be generous enough to accommodate the driver in relative comfort. The same goes for the engine: there is a physical limit to how small an engine of a given capacity can be. The gearbox, too — with all of its ratios to accommodate — can only be so small.

Weight is another key issue in Formula 1 car design. FIA regulations stipulate that the *combined* weight of the car, driver and on-board fluids must at no time fall below 600 kg (1323 lb). To verify that cars comply with this requirement, FIA inspectors undertake spot checks during race meetings. The car is placed on four pressure-sensitive plates, then the driver must stand on another plate for the combined weight of the car and driver to be measured with precise accuracy.

Throughout the design phase there are strenuous efforts to reduce the overall weight of the car. Designers are only too aware that every kilogram over the minimum permissible weight adds about 0.03 second to each lap: 5 kg (11 lb) of excess weight would therefore translate into a 12-second deficit over a typical race distance. The evolution of Formula 1 cars under the current set of regulations is now so advanced that all of the teams manage to build their cars well below the statutory minimum weight, then add slabs of lead ballast to bring them back up to the required level. The lead is placed low down in order to keep the car's centre of gravity as low as possible. Achieving a low centre of gravity is a key objective in the design process because it makes the car more stable under heavy cornering, braking and acceleration forces.

As well as this 'vertical' weight distribution, more even distribution of the car's mass horizontally, between the front and rear sets of wheels, is also crucially important because this allows both sets of tyres to contribute more effectively to the overall performance and handling. Designers strive to bring weight forward as much as possible because the car's heaviest components — the engine, the gearbox and the fuel — are unavoidably concentrated at the rear, placing a proportionately greater burden on the rear tyres. When placing ballast on the cars, not only is it positioned low down, it is also placed well forward, with the result that the centre of gravity of the best Formula 1 cars is probably as close as it is possible to get to the middle.

Tyres are probably the single most important factor in the performance of contemporary Formula 1 cars, with aerodynamics running a close second. The key function of the car's aerodynamic features is to generate downforce, which in turn generates grip. Mechanical — as opposed to aerodynamic — grip is another vitally important quality. This derives from the car's weight distribution and suspension geometry, and the performance of the differential and the tyres.

Blending the aerodynamic and mechanical qualities into a winning package is the goal of all Formula 1 car designers.

THE CHASSIS

WEIGHING just 35 kg (80 lb), a Formula 1 chassis — sometimes called the 'tub' — is a miracle of modern engineering. It is the central structural element of the car, with virtually all of the other load-bearing elements attached directly to it, so it must be capable of withstanding powerful and wildly fluctuating forces imposed from all directions — yet, at the same time, resist any tendency to flex. At the front of the chassis, the front suspension and steering system feed in loads as they react to bumps and undulations in the racetrack surface and respond to high cornering and braking forces. The front aerofoils also feed in massive loads — in this case aerodynamic, as opposed to mechanical loads — via the nosebox, to which the aerofoils are attached.

At the opposite end of the chassis, on its rear face, are the engine mounts. These feed in brutal bending and twisting loads, since this is the structural joint where the front half of the car (the chassis) is attached to the rear half (the engine, with the gearbox, rear suspension and rear aerofoils fixed to the engine to form a single unit).

From the sides, too, the chassis is stressed — because the sidepods are mounted there, and they have powerful flows of air coursing over and through them. Structural loads are even fed into the *underside* of the chassis, by the undertray — an aerodynamic device that creates enormous downforce — and from within the chassis by the seat and safety harness as the driver's body reacts to cornering and braking forces.

0.1099
0.1021
9E-02
9E-02
8E-02
7E-02
6E-02
5E-02
5E-02
4E-02
3E-02
2E-02
2E-02
8E-03
0.0

CHASSIS--FULL LAMINATE W/ BULKHEADS

CARBONFIBRE is the predominant material used in Formula 1 chassis construction, because of its unrivalled strength in relation to its weight.

It is crucially important to the overall performance and handling of the car that the chassis has sufficient stiffness to prevent flexing. Both torsional stiffness (a resistance to twisting loads) and beam stiffness (a resistance to bending loads) are vitally important. Another fundamental design objective is to create sufficient impact resistance, otherwise the car will fail to protect the driver in the event of a major accident. There is a potential conflict between the need for stiffness and the need for impact resistance — because the more stiffness any carbonfibre material has, the more brittle it tends to be. Certain types of carbonfibre are outlawed by the regulations for this reason. They are insufficiently resilient for the Formula 1 environment, and are in the class known as 'high-modulus' carbonfibres.

Chassis designers can partially resolve the conflict between stiffness and resilience by conceiving smoothly flowing shapes that distribute impact loads evenly rather than introducing angular features that concentrate them.

Advanced computing techniques are applied in the design of the chassis. Given the complexity of both the chassis and the forces acting upon it, calculating the most effective way to build a strong, rigid, lightweight structure would be nightmarishly difficult were it not for finite element analysis (FEA). FEA is a computerised method of predicting and analysing the structural characteristics of key components at the design stage with a high degree of accuracy. Although the structural characteristics of a chassis are infinitely complex, by simplifying it into a *finite* number of elements using a computer, it becomes possible to analyse its properties and behaviour under the influence of a wide variety of loads and calculate the most effective way to manufacture it.

FEA software can produce colour-coded images that show the distribution of structural loads and pinpoint where stress concentrations and other potential weak spots will occur, allowing chassis designers to amend their designs accordingly. Both static and dynamic (animated) imagery can be produced. Deformations (flexing) of the chassis can be displayed in such a way that extremely small movements are artificially exaggerated, making it easier to identify the areas where movement is taking place.

Without FEA, a greater margin for error would have to be factored into the chassis construction, and the resulting structure would be heavier than necessary, rendering the car uncompetitive.

Like carbonfibre, FEA had its roots in the aerospace industry and was adopted by Formula 1 designers anxious to find that elusive extra edge. Among the best-known FEA software products employed in Formula 1 is PTC's Pro/MECHANICA, which is used by the Ferrari team.

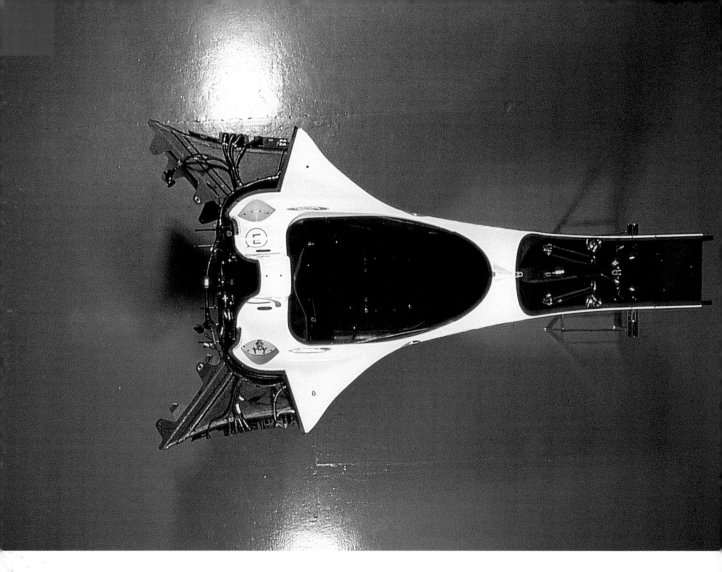

FORMULA 1 chassis have a sandwich construction: a core of aluminium honeycomb is sandwiched by two carbonfibre skins. The skins are composed of many layers of carbonfibre, bonded and compacted together by a curing process (a combination of extreme heat and pressure that turns the pliable fabric rigid). The carbonfibre is known as 'pre-preg', because the carbon fibres are pre-impregnated with an epoxy resin to ensure that the resin is evenly distributed, guaranteeing consistency in the make-up and performance of the finished product once curing has taken place.

All three layers of this sandwich are bonded together with high-integrity adhesive so that they become an integral whole.

Until fairly recently, Formula 1 chassis were manufactured in several pieces and then bonded together, but the process has been refined in the interests of strength, rigidity and weight-reduction, so that a contemporary chassis is virtually a one-piece structure. Some internal stiffening is added in the form of two bulkheads — one immediately behind the driver (the seat-back), the other around his knees (the dash bulkhead).

THE CHASSIS takes longer to manufacture than any other element of the car, so it is the first element to have its design committed.

Before the chassis itself can be manufactured, a full-sized reproduction of it must be produced. This is not a mock-up of the chassis. It is a pattern, or 'buck', from which moulds will be produced in which to lay up the carbonfibre pieces that form the chassis. This is the stage at which CAD becomes CAM, because the same computer software used to design the car now helps with the process of manufacturing it. Data from the CAD system, converted into CNC code (a set of instructions that automated machine tools can understand) are fed into a routing machine. This fashions the chassis pattern from slabs of either a proprietary pattern-making material (such as Ureol) or mahogany.

These slabs are stacked one on top of another and bolted together to produce the chassis pattern.

The moulds for the chassis are made from carbonfibre. To produce the moulds, the chassis pattern is first coated with epoxy paint to protect it from chemical attack by the resins in the carbonfibre. The pattern is ovened to harden the paint, then hand-sanded with very fine wet-or-dry and rubbed with T-Cut to produce a smooth surface finish. A brown, slate powder-based gel coat is then applied to the pattern. This will be the inside surface of the mould when it is eventually pulled from the pattern. Several layers of carbonfibre are then applied to create the mould, and the pattern/mould combination is put through a final process to cure the mould. At this stage the mould is removed from the pattern, which is by this stage redundant.

ONLY NOW can the chassis itself be manufactured. Laying up hundreds of individual pieces of carbonfibre in the chassis moulds is a meticulous and labour-intensive process. Highly skilled laminators closely follow explicit written instructions and diagrams set out by the chassis designers as a result of their earlier FEA work. The number of carbonfibre layers (plies) in each given area of the chassis reflects the loads to which that area will be subjected when the car is driven in anger. Similarly, the angles at which the plies are oriented reflect the way that those loads will be dealt with.

For example, orienting the plies so that the fibres run in one particular direction will transfer loads to a specific part of the chassis. Conversely, multiple plies oriented so the fibres run in a variety of directions distribute loads over a wide area. The orientation of the fibres depends upon whether the loads being dealt with in that region are torsional (twisting), compressive (pushing), or tensile (pulling).

Formula 1 chassis are composed of both woven carbonfibre fabrics and unidirectional (non-woven) carbonfibre tape.

At various stages in the laying-up process, steps are taken to compact the layers of carbonfibre together and force them against the contours of the mould to ensure a faithful reproduction of the intended form. This is achieved by enveloping the mould/lay-up combination in a tailored plastic bag and placing it in an autoclave — a large pressurised chamber in which a combination of heat and vacuum can be applied. The heat softens the resin in the carbonfibre, allowing it to be drawn away through tubes set into the bag and increasing the fibre-to-resin ratio, which in turn dramatically increases the structural performance of the carbonfibre. The vacuum state assists this process, by helping to drive out the excess resin but, more importantly, it also forces the carbonfibre plies against one another, and against the surface of the mould.

This process is known as 'consolidation and debulking'.

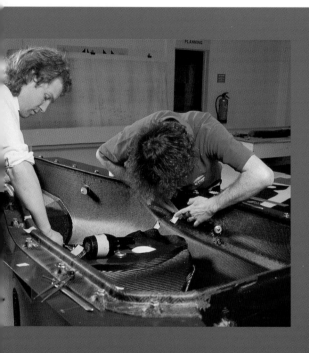

WHEN THE first carbonfibre skin has been completed, the aluminium honeycomb layer is placed on top of it, with a layer of adhesive between them to bond them together. The honeycomb varies in thickness, depending upon the structural demands predicted for particular areas of the chassis by the designers using FEA.

Localised reinforcements known as inserts are set into holes pre-cut in the honeycomb at points where bolts and other types of fastener will pass through the chassis to retain suspension components, and fittings such as those to which the driver's safety harness will be attached. Inserts are typically made from aluminium or a very high-density resin-impregnated fabric material called Tufnol.

Overall, the carbonfibre/aluminium honeycomb sandwich construction is very strong, but it cannot withstand highly localised loads imposed from within its structure. Without the inserts, the chassis walls would simply tear where bolts and other fittings impose loads. The inserts have a wide range of shapes and sizes, depending on the nature of the fittings that are to be attached to them.

When the layer of aluminium honeycomb and inserts has been added, the second skin of carbonfibre is built up on top of it and subjected to the same cycle of autoclaving as the first skin. Although the carbonfibre skins are composed of many plies, they are extremely thin once they have been cured.

All that remains to complete the chassis once it has been prised from its mould is to drill holes through the various inserts. To ensure absolute precision, this is undertaken with a CAD-driven five-axis automated machining rig — so called because the drill bit can move in five different axes. It can translate up and down, in and out, and from side to side, tilt up and down, and skew from side to side.

As well as drilling the holes, the five-axis rig taps and countersinks them as necessary. Locations of holes drilled in the chassis are: on the front face of the chassis, for the fittings that retain the nosebox; on the sides of the chassis, for the sidepod attachments; and on top of the chassis, just in front of the cockpit aperture, for the mountings for the inboard elements of the front suspension.

CRASH-TESTING

2

WHEN Formula 1 cars collide, or an errant car strikes a tyre wall or guard rail at speed, enormous forces are unleashed. Structures collapse, parts fly off in all directions, drivers are violently shaken and sometimes even struck by debris, and their internal organs can be severely jolted, with potentially lethal consequences. Accidents in Formula 1 are inevitable, but sustained efforts to reduce the likelihood of death or serious injury have changed the sport beyond recognition. Teams must prove to the satisfaction of the FIA that their cars meet stringent safety regulations, but this is not merely a paperwork exercise. A dramatic series of impact simulation tests is carried out under the close scrutiny of an FIA inspector to ensure that each and every car on the grid is crashworthy.

There are specialised facilities for such tests. Of these, Cranfield Impact Centre (CIC), part of Cranfield University near Newport Pagnell, England, is the most used. Almost all of the British-based Formula 1 teams undertake their crash-testing there, while the others undertake their crash-testing at facilities on the continent.

Teams pay around $3500 a day to test at Cranfield. All of the photographs of crash-testing in this chapter were taken there, but the other facilities used for Formula 1 crash tests are broadly similar, and the test criteria are identical.

THE FIA-MANDATED crash-testing programme for Formula 1 cars has evolved to simulate as accurately as possible the actual types of crashes that occur in Grands Prix. Some of the tests are *dynamic*, meaning that a car (or a specific part of a car) is smashed against a solid object, or a solid object is smashed against the car. The other tests are *static*, meaning that loads are applied slowly rather than suddenly.

Needless to say, the dynamic tests are the more spectacular, and the 'frontal impact test' is the most spectacular of all. It was formulated to assess two things: the ability of the nosebox to protect the driver's feet and ankles from serious injury; and the ability of the chassis structure in general, and the nosebox in particular, to absorb the kinetic energy of the impact, so that the driver does not experience injurious deceleration forces.

When the 'frontal impact test' is undertaken at Cranfield University, the FIA test criteria are met by propelling a chassis/nosebox combination down an 11-degree ramp with bungee cords. It strikes a steel plate 50 mm (2 in.) thick, which is set in a huge concrete block. The impact speed is 14 metres per second (45.9 feet per second) — slightly over 50 kph (33 mph).

Although such a low speed may seem unrepresentative of a real Formula 1 collision, it should be borne in mind that, in the vast majority of accidents, cars strike obstacles at an oblique angle, not head-on as in the FIA crash test. Also, by the time a car strikes anything of substance, much of its energy will already have been dissipated by friction between the tyres and gravel (or asphalt) in a run-off area, and by reactions of the suspension as the car bounds over the gravel. Furthermore, a length of guardrail and its protective layers of tyres yield considerably. The steel plate used in the FIA crash test, on the other hand, yields *not an inch*!

In the cockpit, an instrumented mannequin stares impassively at the steel plate at the foot of the ramp. The mannequin is *anthropomorphic*, meaning that the articulation of its joints and the masses of its limbs and head replicate those of a real human being. It weighs 75 kg (165 lb), and is strapped firmly into the cockpit with a multi-point safety harness of the type approved for Grand Prix racing. Ensconced in its chest is an accelerometer, to measure the deceleration forces that would be inflicted on the driver at the moment of impact.

The chassis has a fuel cell installed, filled with water rather than fuel (for safety reasons) — and also a loaded fire extinguisher — in order to replicate the structural loads these items would generate in a genuine accident. FIA regulations stipulate that the minimum weight of a car at the start of a Grand Prix must be 780 kg (1716 lb), so the sled to which the chassis is attached for the crash test may have ballast added to bring the total combination up to that weight. Joined to the chassis at the engine mounting points, on the rear face of the chassis, the sled effectively represents the mass of the car aft of the chassis — namely, the engine, gearbox, drivetrain, rear suspension, wheels, brakes, and so on.

POISED AT a predetermined point at the top of the ramp, the bungee cords pulled taut, the chassis/sled combination is held by steel jaws while final instrumentation checks are completed. When everyone present has withdrawn to a safe distance, the sled is released. It literally *flies* down the ramp, being borne on air-bearings instead of wheels (there are four small rollers on the side of the sled which momentarily glance rails on the edges of the ramp, but the run is virtually frictionless, ensuring consistency from one run to the next).

A report akin to a rifle shot resounds around the walls of the test building at the moment of impact. A digital camera records the impact for subsequent analysis by the team. If the car designers' calculations are correct, the nosebox should have deformed progressively, absorbing the energy of the impact. The precise impact speed is measured by photo-electric cells. FIA regulations stipulate that the deceleration forces measured by the accelerometer in the mannequin's chest must not have exceeded 60 G for more than a cumulative total of three milliseconds.

In addition to the accelerometer in the mannequin's chest, there are two accelerometers mounted on the sled. If the average deceleration of the sled has exceeded 40 G, or the first 150 mm (5.9 in.) of nosebox deformation has caused deceleration levels to exceed 5 G, the test has been failed. Furthermore, damage must not extend aft of the nosebox/chassis interface, and the FIA inspector also scrutinises the mountings for the driver's safety harness and fire extinguisher to assess their condition. If any damage has been inflicted at these points, again, the test has been failed.

A separate test, known as the 'nose push-off test', is undertaken to verify that the nosebox will not become detached from the chassis in the event of a major *sideways* impact, denuding the car of its most vital energy-absorbing structure. This is a static test.

TO ENSURE that the driver is properly protected in the event of a rear-end impact, Formula 1 cars are fitted with a deformable structure mounted on the back of the gearbox. It has essentially the same carbon-fibre/aluminium honeycomb sandwich construction as the nosebox, but is somewhat smaller. A 'rear impact test' is conducted to validate its effectiveness. This is very similar to the frontal impact test just described, but this time the car stands still and the impact is simulated by smashing the sled into the back of it.

The sled, weighing 780 kg (1716 lb), replicates the impact of another car striking the car under test. FIA regulations demand that the sled's average deceleration must not exceed 35 G — with a peak value no greater than 60 G for three milliseconds — and that structural damage must not extend beyond the rear axle line.

As with the frontal impact test, a separate (static) test is undertaken to ensure that the gearbox-mounted deformable structure will not detach in a major sideways impact. This test was introduced for the 2002 season.

HEAVY SIDE impacts can have disastrous consequences, particularly when they are inflicted by the nose of another car, so the FIA places stringent demands on lateral crashworthiness. Three 'squeeze tests' are undertaken to ensure that the chassis will protect the driver in the event of three types of sideways impact. These are: a car striking the vehicle at the point where the driver's legs are situated; a car striking where his torso is situated; a car striking where the fuel is stored (in a compartment behind the driver's back).

These are static tests applied to precisely specified points on one side of the chassis. A steel plate is driven slowly inwards against the chassis, which is braced from the opposite side by another steel plate, and anchored firmly at the engine mounting points on the rear face of the chassis. The 'squeeze tests' on the footwell and the fuel compartment each apply a load of 25 kN (2.5 tons), while the load applied to the centre of the chassis, where the driver's torso is situated, is 30 kN (3 tons). FIA regulations stipulate that deformation of the chassis must not exceed 20 mm (0.79 in.) in each of these three tests, and the structure must spring back to within 1 mm (0.0394 in.) of its original shape.

In addition, a *dynamic* side-impact test is conducted. This is to test the special deformable structures that the FIA decrees must be fitted to the sides of the car, low down on the chassis, close to the cockpit aperture. It involves mounting the car sideways at the foot of the ramp used for the earlier dynamic impact tests, then smashing the sled into it. The weight of the sled — 780 kg (1716 lb) — replicates the weight of another car, and the impact speed is 10 metres per second (32.5 feet per second), about 35 kph (21 mph).

The average deceleration of the sled must not exceed 20 G. Damage must be limited to the side-impact absorption structure and not extend to the chassis itself.

ONE OF the most treacherous types of accident that can befall a Formula 1 driver is when his car rolls upside-down. Although such accidents are thankfully rare, the cars must be capable of protecting their occupants in such circumstances. A 'rollover impact test' (a static test) simulates this scenario by imposing an enormous load on the rollover hoop, the structure that protrudes above the cockpit to protect the driver's head and neck from crushing injuries.

Before the test begins, the rollover hoop is anchored firmly in position — but tilted back, and canted slightly to one side. This way, when the load is applied vertically onto the top of the hoop, it will impose forces from the same directions as a genuine rollover accident. A load of 200 kN (20 tons) is applied. The angles at which the rollover hoop is tilted and canted mean that this force is 'split' in three directions: 90 kN (9 tons) downwards, 60 kN (6 tons) rearwards, and 50 kN (5 tons) sideways.

Deformation of the rollover hoop does take place, but this is permissible within FIA-specified limits. Several years ago, Brazilian driver Pedro Diniz was fortunate to escape serious injury when the rollover hoop on his Sauber broke off as the car was flipped upside-down. At that time, the FIA-mandated load for the 'rollover impact test' was 76 kN (7.6 tons). The present requirement for nearly three times that load reflects the seriousness with which Formula 1's ruling body viewed that particular accident.

ANOTHER structure on Formula 1 cars performs essentially the same task as the rollover hoop. It is a heavily reinforced area immediately in front of the cockpit aperture, part of which often takes the form of a triangular protrusion just in front of the cockpit lip. This part of the chassis is subjected to a test similar to that undertaken on the rollover hoop. FIA regulations specify that the top of the driver's crash helmet must be at least 5 cm (1.95 in.) below the imaginary line connecting the front and rear rollover-protection structures.

Even the *underside* of the car must be crashworthy, in order to resist intrusion into the region where the fuel is situated if the car is struck by another car whilst upside-down. In the 'underside impact simulation' — a static test similar to the lateral 'squeeze tests' described earlier — the chassis is mounted on its side and a load of 12.5 kN (1.25 tons) is applied to the underside, near the back. FIA regulations stipulate that deformation of the underside of the chassis must not exceed 20 mm (0.79 in.) in this test, and the structure must spring back to within 1 mm (0.0394 in.) of its original shape.

There is a static test to ensure that the sides of the cockpit offer sufficient protection to the driver, and will not collapse under the force of an impact with another object — such as a flying car in a first-corner mêlée. A 'cockpit rim test' is undertaken, in which two circular steel plates — each measuring 10 cm (3.94 in.) in diameter — are pressed slowly down onto either side of the cockpit aperture by a worm-drive mechanism. The loads are applied at two specified points approximately half-way along the aperture, where the structure is at its weakest.

A force of 10 kN (1 ton) is imposed. Deformation of the cockpit sides must not exceed 20 mm (0.79 in.), and the structure must spring back to within 1 mm (0.0394 in.) of its original shape.

AERODYNAMICS

3

AT ANY SPEED over 160 kph (100 mph) a Formula 1 car could literally 'stick to the ceiling'! That is because its aerodynamic devices generate sufficient downforce — 'negative lift' — to support the weight of the car at those speeds. Downforce is the key to the car's exceptional cornering performance. The aerodynamic devices, performing the opposite function to the wings on an aircraft, press the car down onto the racetrack, greatly increasing the grip of the tyres. The increased grip also boosts the car's braking performance.

Contemporary Formula 1 cars generate over two tons of downforce at top speed, and much of that comes from elements of the car that are invisible to the race spectator, hidden underneath it. When an ordinary roadgoing car negotiates a corner, its lateral grip peaks at a little over 1 G, at which point it begins to slide away. A Formula 1 car, by comparison, can generate as much as 3.5 G in high-speed corners, such is the combined might of aerodynamics and tyres.

Formula 1 cars are, in essence, a 'dirty' shape aerodynamically — because FIA regulations require them to have open bodywork, with the wheels exposed rather than faired in — so the challenge of achieving high levels of aerodynamic efficiency is considerable.

LONG BEFORE a Formula 1 car is built, its performance is predicted — and perfected — in a wind tunnel. A scale model, usually 40 to 50 per cent of the size of the real car, is exhaustively tested to optimise the aerodynamic efficiency. These models are very highly detailed, with every relevant feature of the full-sized car faithfully reproduced in miniature. During the course of testing, many variations on the design are assessed, by modifying the model with interchangeable aerodynamic parts. Aerodynamic effects in different regions of the car tend to be interrelated, so the process is complex and arduous.

The wind tunnel is a carefully controlled environment, but designers must take into account the fact that unpredictable external factors will influence the performance of the full-sized car. On the racetrack, a gust of wind, or turbulence created by the car in front, will upset the car's stability, so the design must be 'fine-tuned' to tolerate these influences.

A decade ago, only a few top teams had their own wind tunnels. In the UK, where the majority of Formula 1 teams are based, most hired one of the wind tunnels available on commercial terms at academic institutions and research establishments, such as the University of Southampton and Cranfield Institute of Technology (now Cranfield University). Today, virtually every team has its own wind tunnel. Jordan, for example, built its facility in 1997 at a cost of $3.8 million. Yet Toyota, when preparing its challenger for the 2002 season, hired volume racing car manufacturer Lola's wind tunnel at Huntingdon, near Cambridge, at a cost of $750 an hour.

The top teams run their wind tunnels 24 hours a day when they are developing a new car, while the teams at the tail end of the grid make do with hiring as little as 50 eight-hour days of wind tunnel time a year.

THE AREA where the model is actually tested is known as the working section, but this is just one small part of the overall facility. Out of sight, far upstream of the working section, a huge fan impels the flow of air that is circulated through the tunnel. The fan has contra-rotating sets of blades to cancel out the swirling effect that would result if they spun in only one direction, helping to ensure that the column of air passing through the tunnel is as free from turbulence as possible. The air travels a considerable distance to reach the working section. It is accelerated just before it gets there by the walls, floor and ceiling converging to form what is termed the contraction nozzle.

After exiting the working section, the airflow is recirculated back through the fan to pass over the model time after time. This helps ensure consistency in the test results, because if fresh air were to be drawn in from outside it would introduce temperature fluctuations, altering the density of the air — and therefore its properties — unpredictably. The aim throughout is to achieve *repeatability* — allowing changes in the performance of the test model to be readily identifiable, and measurable with great accuracy, uncorrupted by variables arising from the operation of the wind tunnel.

When models of aircraft are wind tunnel-tested, they are suspended in the very centre of the working section, in what is termed free-stream air, but racing car models are tested in a way that more faithfully

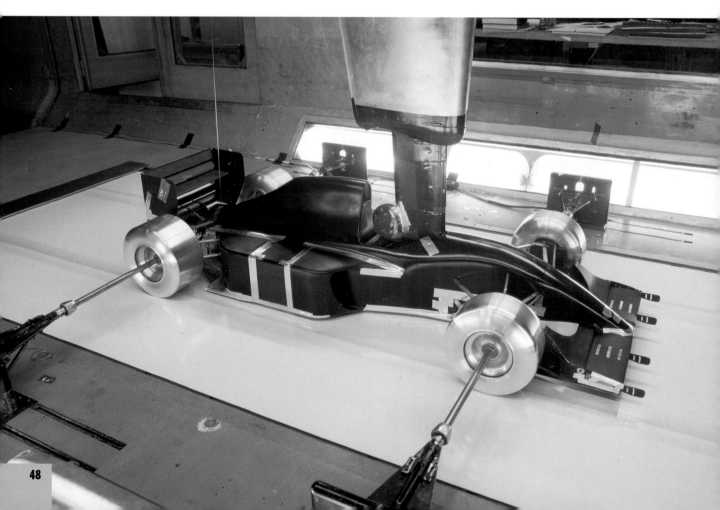

replicates the environment in which racing cars actually operate. They are positioned just above the floor of the working section and, to further enhance the fidelity of the testing, they are suspended above a moving belt that simulates the relative movement of the racetrack surface beneath the car. This 'moving ground' is akin to a conveyor belt, and it moves at the same speed as the airflow passing through the wind tunnel, creating a very realistic environment.

The streamlined strut from which the model is suspended is part of a complex system that measures the aerodynamic forces acting on the model. The resulting data can be viewed on a monitor in the control room overlooking the working section, and are also stored for detailed analysis.

The wheel/tyre units are not actually fixed to the model. They are individually supported on horizontal struts extending from the sides of the working section, and rest on the belt so that they rotate realistically.

During wind tunnel testing, aerodynamicists place particular emphasis on three key performance parameters: downforce, drag and balance.

Continuing advances in technology are altering the nature of aerodynamic testing. In the wind tunnel, laser beams are now being used to measure the airflow at specific points. Lasers offer the benefit of being able to accurately measure the characteristics of the airflow without physically interfering with it.

WIND TUNNEL testing is being increasingly complemented by computational fluid dynamics (CFD) — a method by which the highly complex interaction of airflows around the car can be predicted and analysed mathematically. CFD data are held up for comparison with data gathered during wind tunnel testing, and vice versa, to help validate test results. As well as simulating airflow, CFD can predict the air pressure distribution around the car, and model thermal effects in and around the engine.

As with the FEA structural analysis technique described in Chapter 1, the results of CFD analyses can be presented in a colour-coded form that simplifies interpretation. By far the most used CFD software in Formula 1 is FLUENT.

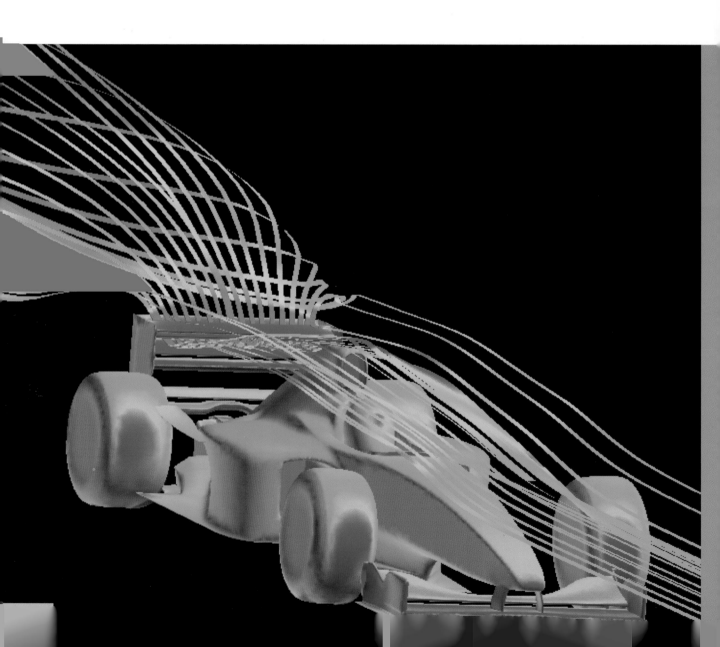

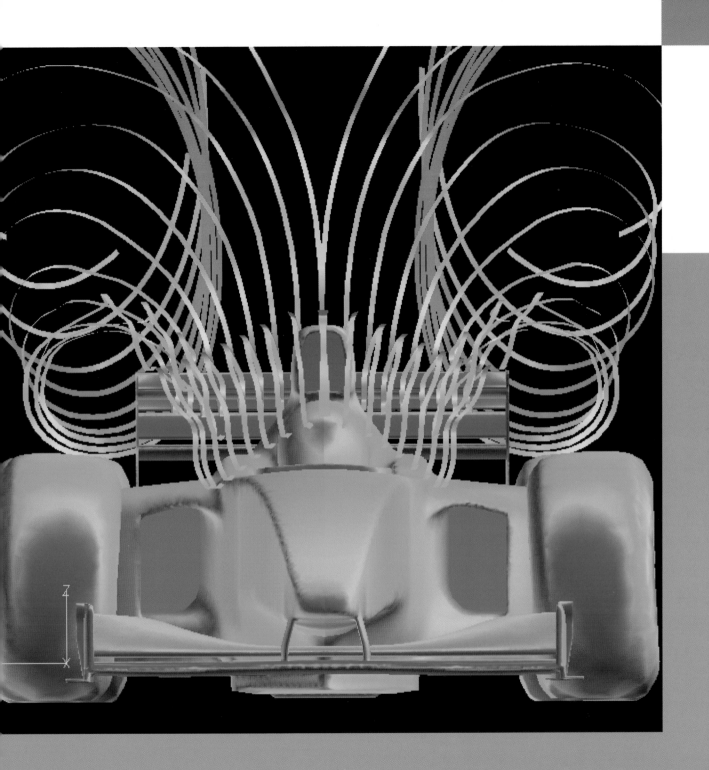

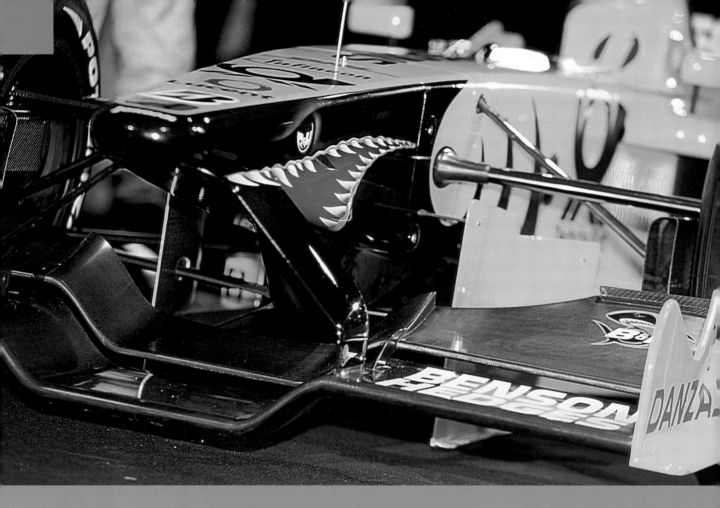

TECHNOLOGY OF THE F1 CAR

AERODYNAMIC devices abound on a modern Formula 1 car. The most visible are the complex arrays of aerofoil surfaces mounted at the front and rear of the car. The front aerofoils typically provide about 25 per cent of the car's total downforce — although as much as 30 per cent can be lost to turbulence when the car is closely following another. The rear aerofoils are capable of generating up to one-third of the car's total downforce.

Downforce levels should increase during the course of a sustained wind tunnel testing programme, as a result of modifications made to the model through constant experimentation. In some cases, however, it is necessary to *reduce* the downforce to increase the car's straight-line speed. This is because drag (air resistance) is another key factor. Drag levels must be kept to an absolute minimum because drag not only restricts the car's speed, but also degrades its fuel economy. Increasing downforce levels often increases drag as well, which is unacceptable. Aerodynamicists must find ways to gain downforce without incurring drag.

Hockenheim and Monza are typical 'low-downforce' circuits. At the opposite extreme, circuits such as the Hungaroring — with its multiplicity of medium-speed corners — requires as much downforce as possible, so most of the cars sport tiny 'winglets' to augment the main aerofoil arrays.

The front and rear aerofoil assemblies comprise many elements. The rear aerofoil ensemble, in particular, has several tiers of aerofoils when it is in a high-downforce configuration. The angles of all of the aerofoil elements are individually adjustable. At their outer extremities, the aerofoil assemblies have endplates that channel the airflow for maximum efficiency by preventing it 'spilling out' from the ends of the aerofoil elements and diminishing their effectiveness.

HIDDEN FROM view beneath the car is its most important aerodynamic device, only seen by spectators when a car is being hoisted high into the air by a crane. It is the undertray: a panel of carbonfibre/aluminium honeycomb sandwich construction, attached directly to the underside of the chassis. It has a flat central 'keel' flanked by two more flat surfaces, elevated 50 mm (1.95 in.) in relation to the 'keel', on either side. The undertray works in conjunction with an upward-sloping 'ramp' at the rear of the car (the rear diffuser) to generate colossal downforce — almost as much as the front and rear aerofoil assemblies combined.

The relationship between the undertray and the rear diffuser is crucial. The diffuser's upward-sloping shape widens the gap between the underside of the car and the racetrack surface, which causes the airflow in that region to slow down in the same way that the flow of water slows down when a river becomes wider. When an airflow is slowed down its pressure increases, so this causes it to be expelled more rapidly from the back of the diffuser. This in turn draws air out from beneath the undertray — accelerating it — and as it does so, the pressure of the air in that region decreases in relation to the air around the rest of the car, creating downforce.

Ride-height — the clearance between the underside of the car and the racetrack surface — has a profound influence on the efficiency of the undertray/rear diffuser combination. The closer the underside of the car is to the racetrack surface, the more downforce is generated. To reduce downforce, thereby reducing the speed of the cars as a safety measure, FIA regulations require the undertray to be fitted with a strip of Jabroc wood 10 mm (0.4 in.) thick. This serves as a 'witness' if the car is run at an illegally low ride-height; if the Jabroc has been worn down to less than 9 mm (0.36 in.) by the end of the race, the car is disqualified.

The car designer's aim is to achieve the *optimum* — as opposed to maximum — level of downforce, because balance is also a key factor in the car's performance. Balance, as the term applies to racing car aerodynamics, means the car's sensitivity to changes in pitch and heave.

Changes in pitch occur when the car adopts a nose-up attitude during acceleration, and a nose-down attitude under braking. These movements cause the car's centre of pressure (the point at which all of the aerodynamic forces acting upon the car are in equilibrium) to shift fore and aft, which destabilises it. A major objective in wind tunnel testing is to both minimise this centre-of-pressure shift and improve the car's tolerance to shifts when they occur.

Changes in heave are vertical translations — changes in ride-height — as the car passes over undulations in the racetrack surface. These also destabilise the car because they cause its downforce levels to vary unpredictably. During wind tunnel testing, computer-controlled servos can alter the model car's pitch angle and ride-height remotely while the wind tunnel is in operation, allowing aerodynamicists to assess the effects of such movements on the car's balance.

Bargeboards — also known as turning vanes — are aerodynamic devices attached to the car's flanks to help control the complex disturbances in the airflow departing the front aerofoils. If left unchecked, these disturbances would diminish the efficiency of other aerodynamic devices situated further back on the car. Different sizes, shapes and combinations of bargeboards are fitted according to the aerodynamic requirements of particular cars at particular circuits. In certain configurations, there are slots in the bargeboards to allow elements of the front suspension to pass through.

In wind tunnel testing prior to the full-sized car being constructed, many different types of bargeboard designs and combinations are assessed — and this activity continues even when the Grand Prix season is underway, because development is a relentless process.

THE ENGINE cover fulfils an important role in the overall aerodynamic performance of the car. The lightweight shroud cloaks the engine and its air inlet duct (snorkel), the gearbox and the rear suspension. It must be as streamlined as possible, so as to allow the airflow to pass smoothly to the rear aerofoil assembly for maximum effect. It must also have the minimum frontal area, in order to reduce drag, so its sweeping shape hugs the contours of the highest points on the engine. At the sides, it flares out gracefully to blend with the shape of the sidepods.

Extensive wind tunnel tests perfect the shape of the engine cover.

THE SIDEPODS house the radiators and 'fill' much of the space between the front and rear wheels with a streamlined structure. Their shape inevitably generates a certain amount of lift. The design process required to define the shape of the sidepods is a good example of the way in which aerodynamic effects in different regions of the car tend to be interrelated, complicating the process considerably. In determining the height of the sidepods, for example, a compromise must be made because they must be tall enough to accommodate the radiators, but they must not be so tall as to interfere with the flow of air over the upper elements of the rear aerofoil assembly.

Sidepod height also influences the flow of air over the car as a whole. The airflow, having passed over the front tyres, must transit the upper surfaces of the sidepods before passing over the rear tyres. The sidepod height has a bearing on the manner in which the airflow changes direction over those three regions, which in turn has a bearing on the total downforce generated by the car, and on the car's stability in pitch and heave.

The complications do not end there. The length of the *undertray* directly influences the length of the sidepods, due to an FIA regulation known as the 'shadowplate ruling'. This stipulates that the sidepods must not extend beyond the perimeter of the undertray, as viewed from above. Yet the length, height and shape of the sidepods have a bearing on the total lift-to-drag ratio of the car — which is a critical factor — so, again, a compromise must be made at the design stage.

Hidden from view within the sidepods, the radiator ducts perform a vital function. They direct the airflow at the radiators to cool the engine. Wind tunnel testing determines the precise size and shape of the radiator ducts. The size must be such that the volume (mass) of air supplied to the radiators is sufficient to provide adequate cooling to the engine, while the shape must be such that the airflow remains smooth on its journey towards the radiators. If the air became turbulent, there would be an uneven distribution of cooling air across the face of each radiator, and the engine would then have a tendency to overheat.

Simply making the radiators larger to compensate for any deficiencies in the radiator duct design is an unacceptable compromise, because having additional radiator area creates additional aerodynamic drag, too — and also extra weight, because the larger the radiator the greater the volume of water being carried.

The radiator ducts have to withstand considerable aerodynamic forces, but do not perform a structural load-bearing function, so they are of an ultra-lightweight, single-skin carbonfibre construction.

ENGINE & TRANSMISSION

CHAPTER

4

A FORMULA 1 car can accelerate from a standstill to 160 kph (100 mph) in just three seconds. It has only half the weight of an average family hatchback, but around ten times the horsepower. This power-to-weight ratio, combined with the most advanced automotive technology, translates into breathtaking performance.

Formula 1 engines typically have around 900 moving parts, and run at speeds as high as 18,000 rpm — generating up to 875 hp. At full throttle, the pistons are subjected to acceleration forces of up to 8500 G. On ultra-fast circuits, the engine can be operating at full throttle for up to 70 per cent of the lap — the car reaching speeds as high as 350 kph (215 mph) on the long straights at Monza. At Indianapolis, along the pit straight and the banked corner that precedes it, the engine runs on continuous full throttle for 24 seconds.

Internal surfaces within the engine can reach temperatures of over 300 degrees C. The engine oil and water normally operate at temperatures of 115–120 degrees C, but in certain circumstances — such as when the car is standing still on the grid — they can soar to 140 degrees C.

It goes without saying that Formula 1 engines are highly stressed! The spectacular sight of an engine expiring in a gigantic plume of white smoke is one that is seen frequently. Although there is very little left in this one, a Formula 1 engine normally holds around 10 litres (18 pints) of specially formulated synthetic oil, of which around 5 litres (9 pints) will be within the crankcase and cylinders at any given time. All of the engines have dry-sump lubrication systems, with high-capacity scavenge pumps changing the oil every 15 seconds. All of the cars carry their engine oil in a thin, flat tank set in a shallow recess in the aft face of the chassis.

FIA REGULATIONS stipulate that Formula 1 engines must have a maximum capacity of 3 litres, with ten cylinders, and they must be normally aspirated. The capacity limit and the prohibition on turbocharging and supercharging are both intended to restrict the power output of the engines in the interests of safety. The limitation on the number of cylinders is intended to keep costs in check, because if one manufacturer fielded an engine with an alternative layout — such as a V8 or flat-12 — and achieved success with it, the others would be compelled to follow suit, resulting in massive cost inflation within the sport.

The regulations governing Formula 1 engine design will remain unchanged until 2007. Manufacturers commit huge sums to the sport, and seek such stability to safeguard their interests. The downside with such restrictive regulation is that the scope for technical diversity is somewhat limited.

When embarking on the design of a Formula 1 engine from scratch, the first steps are to select the bore and stroke, and the angle between the cylinder banks (the vee angle). A series of computer simulations is undertaken to assess the advantages and disadvantages of particular combinations, taking into account such factors as fuel consumption, weight, weight distribution, engine dimensions, and heat-rejection characteristics. Computer-simulation exercises to determine the best configuration for a new engine are conducted in close collaboration with the chassis designers.

Formula 1 engine designers are only too aware that the engine alone does not win a race — the overall package of car and engine working in harmony does. And it is not simply outright horsepower that singles out a superior engine, because that is only one of several key performance parameters that must be optimised. Of equal importance is 'driveability' — the ability of the engine to be tractable in a race situation, so that the driver can accelerate cleanly out of slow corners, tiptoe around them when the track conditions are treacherously wet, and jockey for position when he is surrounded by other cars and his ideal racing line has been compromised.

The *installation* of the engine in the car must also be optimised — partly due to the role the engine plays in the overall weight distribution of the car, but particularly due to its influence on the aerodynamics at the rear of the car. Engine designers make strenuous efforts to keep the engine as compact as possible, so that it leaves more room for the aerodynamic features in the vicinity of the engine. These include the rear diffuser — the upward-sloping 'ramp' at the rear of the undertray that generates vital downforce — and the carbonfibre or titanium channels on either side of the engine which direct air flowing from the radiators out through the back of the car.

Structurally, too, the engine plays an essential role in the overall effectiveness of the car. Attached by a pair of steel or titanium mountings on the sump and either one or two mountings on each camcover, a Formula 1 engine is cantilevered out from the aft face of the chassis as a fully stressed structural member — carrying the gearbox, to which the rear suspension and rear aerofoil assemblies are in turn attached — so it must be very strong and rigid to cope with enormous structural loads, yet also extremely lightweight. Keeping the engine as small as possible, and mounting the engine as low as possible on the chassis, helps lower the car's centre of gravity, and for the same reason the engine itself is designed such that, wherever feasible, mass is distributed low down.

Fuel economy is another vital factor in engine design. A thirsty engine consumes more time on pit stops, requires the car to carry a heavier fuel load and forces more restrictions on race strategy.

Finally — and most importantly of all — the engine must be *reliable*. An engine alone cannot win a race, but it can most certainly lose one…

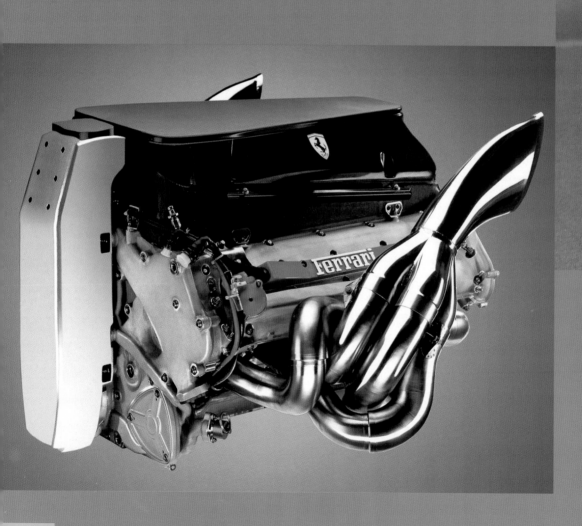

FERRARI is one of only a handful of Formula 1 teams that design and manufacture their powerplants 'in house'. Jaguar, Toyota and Renault also produce their own engines, but their current projects are relatively new. Ferrari stands unique in Formula 1, in having created its own engines for several decades. Beyond this exclusive quartet, the teams source their motive power from further afield, usually by entering into a partnership with a major automobile manufacturer, as McLaren did some years ago with Mercedes-Benz, and BAR and Jordan have done more recently with Honda. In these cases, the relationship is strategic — underpinned by the marketing and research-and-development objectives of the engine manufacturer.

In other cases, teams pay for their engines along more straightforward commercial lines. The Sauber team is one example, obtaining its engines from Ferrari for a huge fee. In all of these cases, the engines are either loaned or leased to teams — rather than donated or sold outright — as engine manufacturers zealously protect the confidentiality of their technological capabilities.

Ferrari's engine design team is led by Paolo Martinelli and Gilles Simon.

TECHNOLOGY OF THE F1 CAR

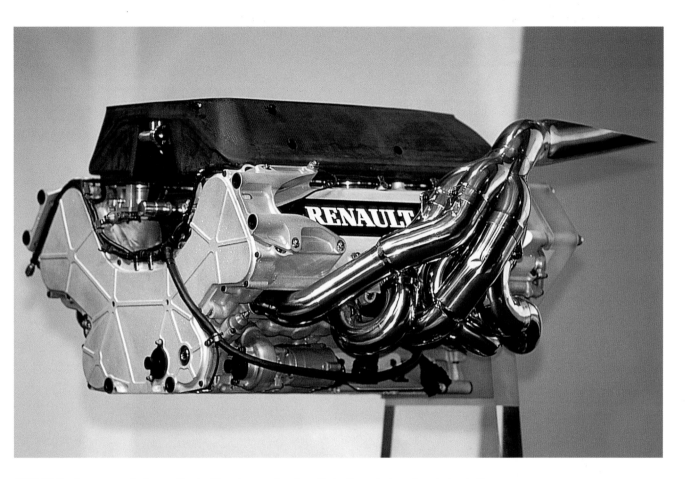

ONE OF the few areas offering really significant scope for diversity in Formula 1 engine design is the selection of the vee angle. The vee angle is a fundamental factor in the overall balancing of an engine, as it allows some of the major out-of-balance forces to be cancelled out. The vee angle also has an important influence on the installation (packaging) of the engine within the car, as it determines how much space is available for other components, where they can and cannot be sited, and how much space is available for aerodynamic features in the vicinity of the engine.

Until recently, the trend was for narrower engines — in the range between 65 and 75 degrees — but now that trend is being reversed. Ferrari, for example, has a 90-degree engine, while Renault has adopted a radical approach, fielding a 111-degree engine. The main benefit of opening out the cylinder banks is that it lowers the engine's centre of gravity. It can also make a better contribution to the structural stiffness of the car. The downside is that it limits the space available for the channels on either side of the engine which direct the air flowing from the radiators out through the back of the car. This 'blockage effect' can compromise the cooling efficiency of the radiators.

MERCEDES-BENZ'S Formula 1 engine — which powers the McLaren — is designed, manufactured and developed by racing engine specialist Ilmor Engineering, based at Brixworth near Northampton in central England. It is very much a corporate 'family affair', as Mercedes-Benz's holding company, Daimler-Chrysler, has a 25 per cent shareholding in Ilmor and a 40 per cent stake in McLaren. Consequently, there is a great deal of knowledge-sharing.

Some idea of the phenomenal level of investment required to compete at the top tier of motor sport can be gauged from the fact that Mercedes-Benz's racing engine contracts account for 85 per cent of Ilmor's annual turnover, which was $122 million in 2000 (the last year for which accounts were available when this book was written). Although Ilmor's work for Mercedes encompasses other single-seater and saloon car racing categories, the Formula 1 programme represents the largest single investment within this figure.

The man at the helm of Ilmor's Formula 1 engine design effort is Swiss-born engineer Mario Illien, a meticulous and innovative thinker. For 2002, Illien has widened the vee angle of the Mercedes engine from 72 to 90 degrees.

A KEY TO getting more power from an engine is enabling it to run at higher revs. Running twice as many revs *theoretically* creates twice as much power because there are twice as many power strokes. But, in fact, this is not a linear process because, as the revs increase, the 'mechanical losses' resulting from friction between the moving parts, excessive inertia, and minute distortions of components under the increased loads being imposed upon them, increase *more* rapidly. So a point of diminishing returns is reached and the power curve plateaus — and, in any case, the risk of a breakage increases dramatically as that point is reached.

The bore exceeds the stroke in all Formula 1 engines, because shorter-stroke engines have the ability to rev higher. There are several reasons for this, one being that shorter conrods are less susceptible to breakage. Also, an increased cylinder diameter creates space for bigger valves.

The BMW engine — generally recognised as the highest-revving engine in Formula 1 — powers the Williams cars. Williams endured a period in the doldrums after the departure of maestro aerodynamicist Adrian Newey in 1997. Then came the partnership with BMW, back in Formula 1 to regain the World Championship-winning prestige it achieved in its previous involvement in motor sport's premier category. The BMW engine's prodigious power output in 2001 — over 850 hp — allowed the Williams to run with larger wing angles without conceding top speed to its competitors.

BMW's input to Williams, like Mercedes-Benz's to McLaren, is not restricted to engine technology. BMW contributes technical input to the development of the Williams gearbox, using lessons learned about materials and machining techniques from its road-car activities. Rumour has it that BMW will also assist in such disparate areas as aerodynamics and suspension development in the near-term future. It is a two-way process, because BMW firmly believes that some of the know-how gained from its Formula 1 programme will find its way into future road-car engines.

THERE ARE limitations, strictly enforced by the FIA, on the types of materials that can be employed in the construction of Formula 1 engines. Mercedes-Benz was one of several manufacturers to suffer when the FIA banned aluminium-beryllium, from which its pistons and cylinder liners were made, for 2002. Some exotic materials — most of which originated in the aerospace industry and tend to be very expensive — are incorporated, but others are outlawed. For example, carbon and aramid fibre-reinforced materials cannot be used for the pistons, cylinder heads and block, and only ferrous metals may be used for the crankshaft and cams.

Exotic materials can offer certain advantages in an engine — saving weight and improving reliability — but the FIA wishes to curb excesses in 'unhelpful' expenditure, taking the view that if one manufacturer made widespread use of such materials, the others would follow suit, so there would be no particular benefit to anybody. When stating its case against aluminium-beryllium, the FIA cited safety as well as cost issues (there are potential health risks when machining it).

Ceramic materials offer certain advantages for areas of the engine that get very hot, but although some Formula 1 engines do contain a few ceramic components, the theoretical benefits are often outweighed by drawbacks. The beneficial properties of ceramics include their resistance to temperature-induced expansion and contraction: in fact, their dimensions hardly fluctuate at all. While that makes them capable of maintaining close tolerances at very high temperatures, they are difficult to actually incorporate alongside metal components — because the very fact that their expansion and contraction characteristics *are* so different makes them incompatible.

Carbons and other composite materials often present a similar dilemma: they are theoretically better, but in reality there are enormous difficulties involved in using them in engines, particularly in fixing them to metal components.

Some advanced materials — such as metal-matrix composites (MMCs), which are metals mixed with non-metallic elements such as carbon fibres — go some way towards achieving the best of both worlds, because they offer a *combination* of properties. The little pieces of fibre in the metal help to reinforce the construction, or can add strength in a particular direction, allowing less material to be used and thereby saving weight.

The extent to which exotic materials are incorporated into Formula 1 engines must be put into perspective. Typically, almost two-thirds of the components are made of aluminium, while almost one-third are made of steel. Only approximately five per cent of the components are made from other materials — and those materials include titanium, magnesium and carbonfibre, which can hardly be considered 'exotic' by modern standards — so the proportion of new-breed materials is actually very small. The most significant single contributor to engine materials technology over the past few years has been the improvement in such manufacturing techniques as casting and surface treatment.

FOR THROTTLE operation, Formula 1 cars have electronic 'fly-by-wire' systems in which there is no physical connection between the throttle pedal and the engine. The driver still depresses the pedal against a return spring in the time-honoured manner, but instead of this physically pulling a throttle cable, an electronic sensor known as a potentiometer, installed in the pedal mechanism, tells the engine's electronic control system where the pedal is within its arc of movement, in response to which the throttle actuators are operated remotely — usually by means of hydraulics.

The advantage this offers is that there no longer needs to be a uniform relationship between the throttle pedal movement and the movement of the throttles themselves, so changes can be made to the throttle characteristics to suit the unique combination of the racetrack conditions and the driver's preferred driving style. These changes are made via software, and can be undertaken during the time available between race meetings, or during intervals in testing, practice or qualifying.

It is impossible to over-rev a Formula 1 engine, because the software prevents this.

Pictured here is a Honda engine. The Japanese manufacturer returned as an engine supplier in Formula 1 with the BAR team in 2000, and then added Jordan to its line-up for 2001. Honda is said to have increased the vee angle of its engine from 90 to 96 degrees for the 2002 season.

FORD CONTINUES its long involvement in Formula 1 with the Jaguar team and engine specialist Cosworth Racing, both of which it owns. It also supplies its engine — which has a vee angle of 72 degrees — to the Arrows team. Providing engines to another team can pay technical dividends as well as financial ones, because a greater amount of testing and race mileage can be accumulated in a given timeframe, hastening the engine development programme.

Jaguar's much-publicised arrival in Formula 1 in 2000 was lacklustre, so triple world drivers' champion and erstwhile airline boss Niki Lauda was drafted into the team the following year to provide focus and direction. A great deal is expected of this historic marque, and the board of directors in Detroit will not accept anything less than a world constructors' championship for their mammoth ($100 million a year) investment.

Double over-head camshaft (DOHC) systems and pneumatic valve actuation have been universal in Formula 1 in recent years, but Renault is said to be developing a cam-less engine, so other manufacturers are likely to follow their example. Pneumatic valve control — in which compressed air is used to operate the valves, instead of potentially fragile springs — was another 'first' for Renault, introduced in the quest for higher revs.

All Formula 1 engines currently have gear-driven camshafts (supplanting chain-driven timing systems, which had become increasingly unreliable as engine development caused revs to edge progressively higher).

AS WELL AS serving its own needs, Ferrari supplies engines to the Swiss-based Sauber team, for a reputed $15 million annual leasing fee. Although it is essentially the same engine as that installed in the factory Ferraris, it is badged for Sauber's title sponsor — the Malaysian state petrochemical corporation, Petronas.

The Sauber team, based at Hinwil, achieved huge success in international sports-prototype racing before graduating to Formula 1 in 1993. It has yet to win a Grand Prix, but has performed very respectably and launched the Formula 1 careers of several top drivers, including Heinz-Harald Frentzen and Kimi Räikkönen. The 2001-model Sauber was designed by Sergio Rinland, but he left the team soon after. For 2002, Sauber's Technical Director is Willy Rampf.

Until recently, Sauber was not the only team to run a Ferrari engine in Formula 1. The Prost team was also supplied with the legendary Italian powerplant in 2001 — but, alas, has fared less well. As this book went to press the French team was bankrupt.

THIS IS the Asiatech engine, being used in 2002 by the Italian-based Minardi team. The Asiatech concern is run by a group of Asian investors who acquired the design, manufacturing and development rights to the engine originally produced by Peugeot, but abandoned by the French automobile manufacturer when it quit Formula 1 at the end of the 2000 season. It is the least powerful engine in Formula 1, outputting around 750 hp.

Minardi, frankly, deserves better. The feisty team from Faenza is owned by Australian airline boss Paul Stoddart, whose organisation also boasts impressive technical facilities in Ledbury, England. With more horsepower, Minardi could embarrass much better-funded teams. Its chassis is excellent, and there is no question that the little Italian outfit — which has always punched above its weight — is destined for greater things in the future.

TOYOTA'S ENGINE is reckoned to be very good indeed. The Japanese newcomer to Formula 1 has a mountain to climb, but few would dismiss its chances of ultimate success, given its previous record in other classes of motor sport. Toyota has committed well over $1 billion to its Formula 1 project over the next three years. Headed by Swede Ove Andersson, a former international rallying superstar, the team is based in Cologne, Germany, and has Finn Mika Salo and Scot Allan McNish driving.

Basing the team in Germany, well away from Formula 1's traditional stamping grounds, is a huge risk. There are historical reasons for this: Toyota's motor sport arm already had a thriving facility there. But that is not Toyota's biggest gamble. It is the decision to field a car designed and built totally 'in house' — chassis, engine and gearbox. Only Ferrari — funded by the vast Fiat empire and established over many, many years — currently does this. Renault cannot quite claim the same status, as its chassis has Benetton lineage — and the same goes for Jaguar, which was built upon the foundations of the Stewart team.

Technical Director of Toyota is Gustav Brunner, a German with ample experience and an excellent reputation. There were setbacks before the 2002 season even started. The team's wind tunnel was not in operation in time to be of use in designing this year's car, but this will be a 'learning year' in any case. For 2003, the prospects will be much brighter.

WHEELSPIN is still seen in Formula 1, but to a much lesser degree than in the past. The reason is that FIA regulations now permit traction-control programs to be installed in the cars' electronic control systems, so as to optimise traction in all phases of acceleration. Many argue that this has negated one of the key skills necessary to drive a very high performance car to its limits — deft control of the throttle pedal. Others argue that the really talented drivers will always rise to the top of the pile, regardless of the technology at their disposal.

There are several ways of controlling wheelspin. One relatively simple method is to measure the rotational speed of the front wheels — which, by regulation, are undriven — and electronically impede the combustion cycle of the engine to ensure that the rotational speed of the rear wheels matches that of the front wheels at all times.

Although traction control was prohibited for several years, the FIA found it impossible to police the regulation effectively, and suspicion of cheating was widespread. The FIA's difficulty lay in the fact that electronic engine management systems had become so complex that it was possible for teams to 'disguise' a traction-control function deep within the software, where it became indistinguishable from other, perfectly legal, functions. In order to create a 'level playing field', traction control was legalised during the course of the 2001 season.

urobet.com

ENTERING a corner, the driver has lifted his foot off the throttle pedal. The engine is now on the 'over-run' — retarding the car rather than accelerating it — and the flames belching from its exhaust pipes are the result of unburned combustion products being ignited by the intensely hot pipes.

The exhaust system plays a crucial role in the performance of the engine. It does much more than simply expel spent gases from the engine after each combustion cycle...

A single piston travelling within a ten-cylinder, 3-litre engine should theoretically draw in one-third of a litre of air on the induction stroke — but, *in fact,* despite forced-induction systems (such as turbocharging and supercharging) being prohibited, a highly efficient Formula 1 engine draws in much more air than that. And by cramming more air in, a proportionate amount more fuel can also be squirted in — creating more power.

This 'quart into a pint pot' effect is a fundamental aspect of engine tuning. It is achieved by exploiting the pressure waves generated within the engine by the combustion cycle, ensuring that they arrive at just the right times to draw extra air in before the valves snap shut and the pistons pummel upwards. These pressure pulses travel at the speed of sound and are strongly influenced by the harmonics of the exhaust system. By carefully adjusting the lengths of the exhaust pipes, the harmonics can be altered — in much the same way that organ pipes create specific sound frequencies according to their lengths.

The distance from the valve down to the end of the tailpipe is critical to the exhaust pipe tuning. The complex 'spaghetti' of pipes seen sprouting from the engine results from the need to achieve specific pipe lengths, whilst at the same time minimising the severity of performance-sapping bends by incorporating smoothly curving transitions from end to end — whilst also tucking the exhaust system away as neatly as possible to leave more room for the channels that run downstream of the radiators.

Tailpipes now protrude from the upper decking of the cars, rather than exiting at the rear of the car as they did in the past. This is because irregular inputs of high-energy exhaust gases into the vicinity of the rear diffuser — fluctuating wildly as the driver operated the throttle pedal — tended to unsettle the car aerodynamically. Also, diverting the pipes upwards creates more room for the channels on either side of the engine. Space is already at a premium in that vicinity, because the bodywork of the car tapers in, 'Coke bottle'-style, to fit between the rear wheels.

TINY SENSORS installed in the outer ends of both exhaust manifolds continuously sample the oxygen content of the engine emissions. Known as Lambda sensors, they relay data directly to the engine management system, which adjusts the air-to-fuel ratio accordingly to ensure complete combustion.

Although the final shape of the exhaust system is decided by the car designers, the length and diameter of the pipes is decided by the engine-maker. Formula 1 exhaust systems are made from either Inconel (a heat-resistant alloy originally developed for the aerospace industry, and commonly used in aero-engines) or stainless steel. On occasion, exhaust pipes are manufactured in one piece, rather than being fabricated in several segments.

JUST AS the distance from the valve down to the end of the tailpipe is critical to the exhaust pipe tuning, so the same principle applies to the air inlet ports. Here, the distance from the valve up to the inlet trumpet lip is the critical measurement for tuning.

All of the current Formula 1 engines have four valves per cylinder, and many have variable inlet trumpets. These allow the inlet tract to telescope in synchronisation with the engine revs, maintaining the optimum tuned length throughout the rev range.

The *disadvantage* of variable trumpets is that their operating mechanism adds weight to the top of the engine, raising its centre of gravity, and also adds bulk which can compromise the car designers' efforts to have a low, neatly sculpted engine cover. The trumpets themselves are made of either aluminium — highly polished — or carbonfibre, while the lightweight structure that surrounds them, the trumpet tray, is made of carbonfibre.

The ambient air pressure and temperature have a significant influence on the engine's performance. In very hot weather, or at circuits situated well above sea level, the engine does not perform as well as it does at lower altitudes and temperatures.

Engine development is relentless. Manufacturers are constantly working to improve the airflow into the engine and the passage of gases through it.

To attain its maximum performance the engine must be able to induct the volume of air it needs, and do so efficiently. Great care is therefore necessary when determining the shape of the air inlet duct, or

snorkel: the elegantly curved carbonfibre tunnel that channels air down from the streamlined aperture in the rollover hoop and delivers it to the trumpet tray.

When a car is being designed, the engine's breathing needs — more formally termed the air mass flow requirement — must be fully catered for, and it is important to ensure not only that the correct volume of air will be delivered to the inlet ports, but also that it will be delivered as free from turbulence as possible, so all of the cylinders receive an equal supply.

The snorkel does more than simply channel air to the engine. By having a shape that progressively widens downstream of the frontal opening, it slows down the incoming air in the same way that the flow of water slows down when a river becomes wider. When an airflow slows down, its pressure increases — and this effectively creates a form of forced induction into the engine.

When determining the shape of the snorkel, the designer is faced with a compromise, because it must be fitted within the tight confines of the engine cover — the shape of which is critical to the overall aerodynamic efficiency of the car, particularly the efficient functioning of the rear aerofoil assemblies. It is also very important to ensure that the driver's helmet will not interfere with the flow of air into the snorkel. Several years ago, before proper attention was given to this problem, some drivers had to tilt their heads to one side on long straights to improve the path for the incoming air!

To perfect the design of the snorkel, wind tunnel testing and computational fluid dynamics (CFD) studies are combined with actual engine tests on a dynamometer, using a powerful fan to flow air into the snorkel.

COOLING a Formula 1 engine is a major challenge. The size and shape of the radiators are refined during wind tunnel testing, as they have a major influence on the aerodynamic performance of the car — due to their impeding effect on the airflow — as well as the performance of the engine.

The engine water and oil are cooled by means of radiators mounted in the sidepods. Some cars have a symmetrical arrangement with 'split' water and oil radiators on either side. Others have an asymmetric arrangement with a water radiator on one side and 'split' water and oil radiators on the other. Designers aim to have the minimum amount of pipework, in order to save weight.

On the starting grid, the engine is cooled by installing fans in the entrances to the sidepods and the air inlet snorkel.

Designers are constantly striving to reduce the size of the radiators in order to reduce the car's aerodynamic drag, and also to reduce the overall weight of the car, because the less radiator volume there is, the smaller the quantities of water and oil being carried. The radiators have themselves become progressively lighter over recent years, thanks to improved manufacturing techniques.

Increasingly, Formula 1 engine manufacturers are designing their engines to 'run hotter' so that the size of the radiators can be reduced. They do this not only by improving the heat-rejection capabilities of the engine itself — by achieving a more efficient use of the flow of cooling water through the engine block and cylinder heads — but also by preventing excessive heat build-up from occurring in the first place, by designing the engine's internals so that undue oil agitation is avoided.

This is certainly an attractive route to take, because although engines tend to produce less power the hotter they become, the aerodynamic advantages alone outweigh the slight loss of horsepower. However, diminishing the radiator size can pose problems. When a driver spins his car, the sudden increase in temperature when air ceases to flow through the radiators poses a far higher risk of causing damage when engine cooling is already marginal. Also, if the cooling water gets too hot, it will boil. To prevent this, the FIA mandates the incorporation of a pressure relief valve, set at 3.5 bar, in the water cooling system.

REFUELLING was reintroduced to Formula 1 in 1994, adding a whole new dimension to race strategy. Teams must decide whether to undertake one, two or even three pit stops — and, just as importantly, *when*! The refuelling strategy must not only take into account the time spent actually taking fuel on board, but also the time spent driving into and out of the pits, and the burden of carrying more fuel than necessary at any given point in the race. The latter has a profound effect on the car's pace: every 10 kg (22 lb) of fuel carried adds half-a-second to a typical lap time.

The pit lane refuelling rigs are manufactured under exclusive licence to the FIA by Intertechnique, a French company with a strong aerospace background. The rigs are pressurised and have a capacity of 200 litres (44 gallons).

Following the reintroduction of refuelling, the single most significant impact on the design of the cars was that they became physically smaller, as they no longer have to carry enough fuel to complete the full race distance.

Formula 1 engines would not win any prizes for fuel economy. Consumption can be as high as 1.4 km to the litre (4 miles to the gallon) — so during the Monaco Grand Prix, for example, which covers 262 km (163 miles), a car might consume as much as 187 litres (41 gallons) of fuel.

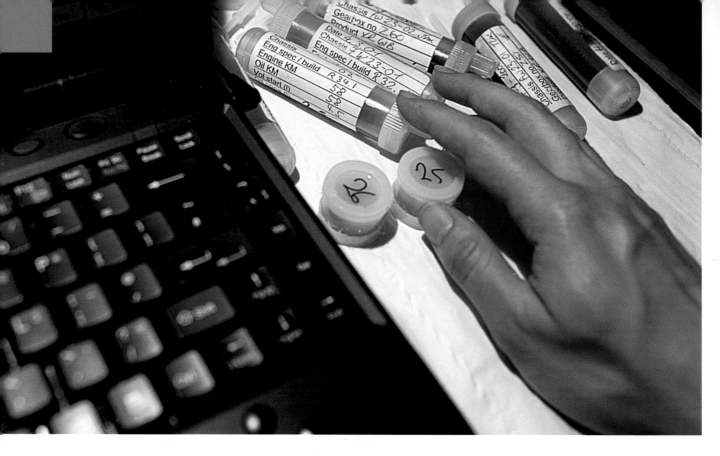

FORMULA 1 engines are fuel-injected, and FIA regulations decree that they must run on unleaded petroleum. Although the rules require the fuel to be of 'street standard', it is specially concocted to maximise its performance to the uppermost limit. In actual fact, there is very little performance gain from the painstaking effort of special processing but Formula 1 is so competitive that teams must exploit every single opportunity, however small, to maintain their competitive edge. FIA inspectors police the fuel regulations very strictly, as this is an area where teams could readily gain an illegal advantage. The fuel must contain the same components used in roadgoing car fuels, and in similar concentrations — and must be pre-approved before the team can use it.

Employing advanced techniques such as gas chromatography and mass spectrometry, FIA inspectors measure the lead, sulphur and benzene content, distillation and density of the fuel batch, producing a unique 'footprint' of the fuel, which must be matched exactly when samples are subsequently taken at random for analysis during race meetings. There are draconian penalties for transgressors.

FIA regulations specify that the car's entire fuel load must be carried in an approved safety cell, behind the driver, so it is encased immediately behind the seat-back bulkhead — close to the middle of the car, so as to optimise the car's weight distribution. To support it against the harsh manoeuvring of the car, the cell is firmly anchored to the chassis at several points.

Fuel is loaded into the cell through a self-sealing valve recessed into the side of the car and mated to the chassis structure. The valve can be mounted on either side of the car, depending on whether the race is to be run in a clockwise or anticlockwise direction, so it will be on the side closest to the pit garage. The valve is protected — and streamlined — by a hinged, hydraulically activated carbonfibre cover that opens and closes automatically when the car is in the pit lane (it is triggered when the pit lane speed limiter is engaged).

MOST FORMULA 1 cells can hold around 150 litres (33 gallons) of fuel if they are topped up very carefully. However, due to the frantic rate at which they are refuelled during a race, air is trapped at the top of the cell, reducing its capacity to around 120 litres (26 gallons).

The fuel cell is designed to deform if it sustains a major impact, rather than rupture, causing a fire. Special materials and construction techniques are required for an ultra-lightweight structure to achieve this resilience: a fuel cell, less internal fittings, typically weighs just 5 kg (11 lb).

The cells are usually made from a high-performance, puncture- and tear-resistant fabric such as Kevlar, coated with a fuel-resistant elastomer (a rubber-like, flexible, stretchable material). This material is immensely strong — stronger than steel. An inch-wide strip, 2 mm thick, could lift the whole car, complete with its driver and a full fuel load, and still have strength to spare!

A car designer's aim is to ensure that the made-to-measure cell occupies the smallest possible volumetric space within the chassis. When calculating the car's weight distribution, he must also take into account the changing weight of the fuel load during the course of a race. The shape of the fuel cell should be such that the fuel pick-up is constant, and does not allow fuel to become 'stranded' out of reach of the lift pumps.

To ensure that the last remnants of fuel can be scavenged by the lift pumps — and to control the

sloshing of the fuel under cornering, acceleration and braking forces — baffles and 'traps' are incorporated within the cell.

The lift pumps are electrically driven and are mounted in the corners of the fuel cell. The pumps deliver the fuel to a cylindrical carbonfibre receptacle known as a collector, housed within the cell, which offers a constant supply to the main fuel pump that feeds the engine — and is, in turn, driven by the engine by means of a shaft.

On the opposite side of the fuel cell to the refuelling valve in use, covered by a streamlined fairing, there is a carbonfibre plate — mated to the chassis structure — carrying two valves. One valve allows fuel to be loaded much more slowly than it is in a pit stop, so more fuel can be put in. The other valve allows fuel to be delivered directly to the engine, bypassing the fuel cell, so engine technicians can test-run the engine without depleting the on-board fuel level.

The fuel outlet to the engine is situated on the back of the cell. This incorporates a breakaway safety coupling that would prevent fuel from flowing out of the cell and posing a fire risk if the engine became detached from the chassis in a very violent accident. Also on the back of the fuel cell is the air vent valve (a one-way valve that lets air in, but stops fuel getting out).

A Formula 1 fuel cell, complete with all internal fittings, costs around $17,000.

TECHNOLOGY OF THE F1 CAR

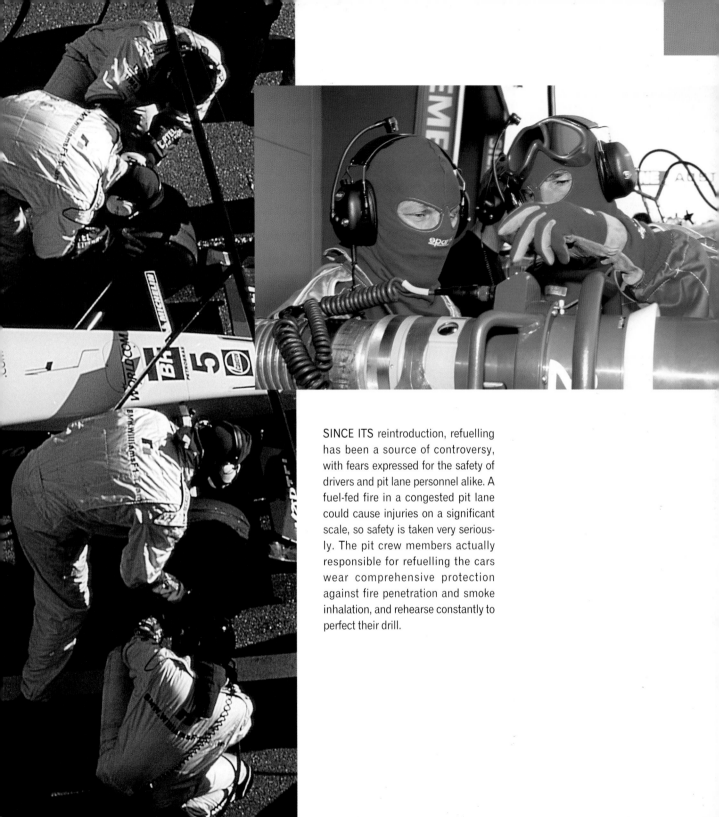

SINCE ITS reintroduction, refuelling has been a source of controversy, with fears expressed for the safety of drivers and pit lane personnel alike. A fuel-fed fire in a congested pit lane could cause injuries on a significant scale, so safety is taken very seriously. The pit crew members actually responsible for refuelling the cars wear comprehensive protection against fire penetration and smoke inhalation, and rehearse constantly to perfect their drill.

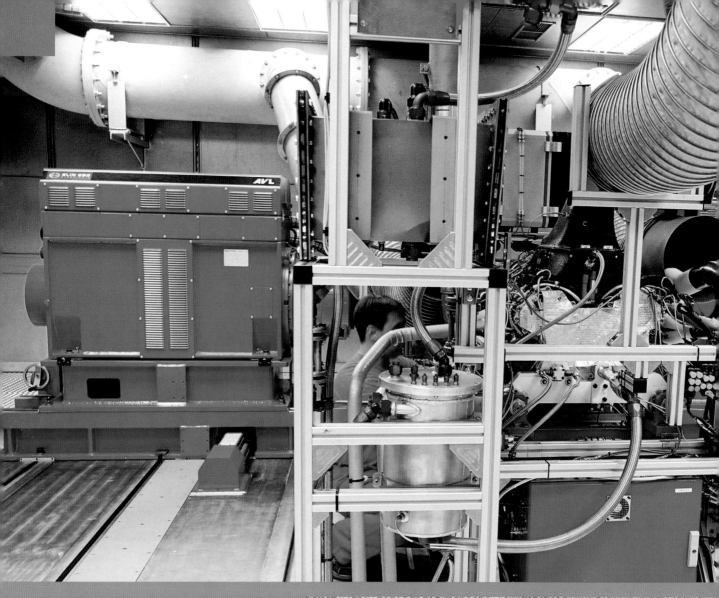

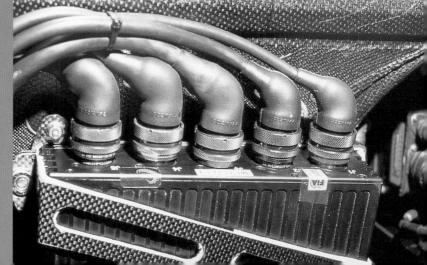

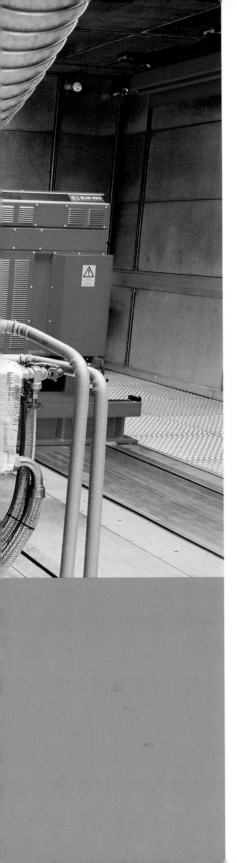

FORMULA 1 engines are completely stripped and rebuilt between uses, then tested on a dynamometer. A rebuild takes approximately 200 hours. Typically, the engine first undergoes a very carefully controlled running-in period on the 'dyno', after which it is put through a setting-up procedure which optimises the delivery of fuel into the cylinders, and the ignition, for that particular engine. A power-curve test is then undertaken, to ensure that the engine runs properly all the way up to maximum revs. The engine is then removed from the dynamometer and undergoes the best part of a day of further checks to make sure that any fault that may have arisen during running, but escaped detection, is duly identified and remedied.

The engine is then fitted to the car, and typically has a 'life' of up to 500 km (310 miles) before being removed, stripped and rebuilt once more.

As well as testing rebuilt engines, dynamometers are used in the relentless drive to develop modifications that give better engine performance. Engines are also tested on 'transient' dynamometers. These are equipped to accurately simulate actual race conditions, such as heat and humidity, rather than testing engines in a sterile laboratory environment.

Typically, a Formula 1 team takes ten engines to a race meeting.

The siting of engine ancillaries and electrical components is partly dictated by the weight distribution objectives for the car as a whole, but mainly by the availability of space within the confines of the car's interior. For example, on some cars the alternator is placed in the vee between the cylinder banks, where it may have to vie for space with assorted elements of the water, fuel, hydraulic and pneumatic systems — and also, in some cases, the throttle actuators and variable-trumpet actuators.

Components and their associated electrical wiring can also be squeezed into the gap between the top of the chassis and the underside of the engine air inlet snorkel, in the narrow space between the radiator ducts and the sidepods, in gaps between the chassis sides and the radiator ducts, and even inside the cockpit. Electronic components are mounted on rubber fittings to insulate them from excessive vibration, and the routing of wires must be such that there is sufficient clearance to avoid chafing

The electrical system of a Formula 1 car is extremely complex, comprising engine ancillaries, processors, sensors, and data-acquisition 'black boxes', linked together by high-integrity electrical cabling with multi-pin plugs. A car typically has over a mile of cabling installed within it. The electrical system is 'ruggedised', the cabling encapsulated in protective sheathing, to withstand operating in conditions where heat, vibration and moisture would cause conventional systems to fail.

Software engineers now outnumber mechanics at races — as many as 20 are taken by the top teams, and the number is rising. For the 2002 season, the FIA legalised systems that allow teams to telemeter signals to their cars — for example, to alter the fuel mixture and the gearchange timing. Prior to this ruling, the cars could relay data to the team, but the process was strictly one-way. The sport's governing body was concerned that two-way telemetry, which had been permissible some years earlier, would allow teams to effectively 'drive' their cars remotely. Finally, though, this prohibition proved impossible to enforce effectively, and so — as with traction control — the legislation was swept aside.

THE CLUTCH is the vital link between the engine and the racetrack — the key to channelling all that horsepower to the tyres. The acid test of a clutch is the frantic sprint off the start line, when the red lights go out and the car accelerates from a standstill to breakneck speeds with savage force. Starts today in Formula 1 are arguably the most important stage in the race, providing an opportunity for drivers to gain places in a few seconds that might otherwise take two hours of painstaking work during the course of the rest of the race. As the entire power of the engine is transmitted through them, the clutch plates are jolted from rest to rotational speeds as high as 18,000 rpm almost instantaneously, subjecting them to temperatures as high as 600 degrees C.

Like many other components in Formula 1, clutches have become ever smaller and lighter because this reduces inertia, improving engine power and responsiveness.

Formula 1 clutch plates are made of carbon-carbon (carbonfibre amalgamated with carbon). It is ideal for this application, because — apart from being relatively lightweight — when subjected to extreme heat, it does not melt, distort, or expand in the way most materials do. Another advantage is that its friction levels do not degrade when it gets very hot. On the contrary, its friction generally increases with temperature, so the harder it is used the better it performs!

No two teams share an identical clutch specification — each demands a slightly different variation to suit its own very precise requirements. But what every unit has in common is outstanding compactness and efficiency. It weighs just 1.2 kg (2.6 lb), with an outer casing machined from titanium for lightness combined with strength. It measures less than 125 mm (5 in.) in diameter and less than 100 mm (4 in.) in length, yet it can transmit over 850 hp.

Clutch plates glow red hot in a good start. The design of the clutch must be such that this heat is dissipated before it can be conducted to the less hardy components surrounding it. As well as the start itself, the clutch must perform efficiently during the practice start off the dummy grid, and during pit stop departures — and also in a restart, if one is called for.

Until a few years ago, Formula 1 clutches were fitted to the rear of the engine, but now they are mounted on the front of the gearbox. This development was primarily driven by engine designers keen to shed the unwelcome weight and inertia of the clutch from the ultra-lightweight crankshafts they were so painstakingly crafting. It did, however, offer significant benefits for clutch performance. For one thing, the gearbox is a much kinder environment than the engine for housing a clutch, because heat and vibration are the primary causes of clutch failure.

All but one Formula 1 team use clutches supplied by the British manufacturer, AP Racing. Sauber, uniquely, is supplied by the German manufacturer, Sachs.

Like the engine, the gearbox is a fully-stressed structural element of a Formula 1 car. Affixed to the rear of the engine, it is part of the 'backbone' of the car, with the rear suspension and the rear aerofoil assemblies mounted directly onto it. Limiting weight is a particularly important factor in gearbox design because, being sited so far back, the gearbox exerts a proportionately greater influence on the weight distribution and handling of the car. Not surprisingly, Formula 1 teams have gone to great lengths to incorporate hitherto unused, lightweight, materials into their gearboxes.

Over the past few years, three teams — Arrows, Ferrari and Minardi — have stood out from the rest in employing cutting-edge materials in the manufacture of their gearbox casings. Arrows has used carbonfibre (locally reinforced by titanium plates and fittings), having pioneered its use for this application in 1998. Ferrari has used fabricated titanium with a carbonfibre front end (where the clutch is housed), while Minardi has used cast titanium. All of the other teams have used either cast magnesium or cast aluminium.

In an effort to reduce the weight of the gearbox as much as possible, designers could be tempted to reduce the gearbox wall thickness, but if the thickness were reduced too much there would be major problems when the car ran. The gearbox would not be rigid enough to prevent it flexing under the high structural loads fed in from the rear suspension and rear aerofoil assemblies. Such flexing would, at the very least, adversely affect the car's handling. It would also degrade the efficiency of the gear ratios within, which run to minute tolerances. At worst, the gearbox would seize completely. A design compromise must therefore be reached, paring weight whilst maintaining stiffness. Extensive use is made of integral bulkheads within the gearbox casing to increase its rigidity.

Cast titanium looks set to become the standard material for Formula 1 gearboxes. Titanium is much lighter than the materials from which gearboxes were traditionally manufactured, but it is very expensive and poses considerable problems in the casting process, so fabrication was the only means by which it could be used in this application. Ways have now been developed to overcome these difficulties, opening the way for more widespread utilisation. Ferrari and Minardi are believed to be fielding titanium gearboxes for the 2002 season.

A key benefit of cast titanium gearboxes is that, being smaller than their conventional counterparts, they gift more room to the rear diffuser.

Almost all contemporary Formula 1 cars have seven-speed gearboxes, and FIA regulations demand that there must be a single reverse gear. Furthermore, the cars must have a drive-disengagement mechanism, so they can be moved more easily if they are abandoned at the trackside. This is activated by a button in the cockpit, the location of which is denoted externally by an 'N' (for 'Neutral') symbol.

All of the current-generation Formula 1 cars have longitudinal gearboxes, as this layout facilitates a narrower gearbox casing than is possible with a transverse gearbox, leaving more space for the rear diffuser. All of the gears are clustered ahead of the rear axle line, thereby keeping their mass within the wheelbase, which improves the car's weight distribution, enhancing its handling characteristics.

Formula 1 gear ratios are made of high-alloy, low-carbon steel — a very resilient metal offering excellent resistance to wear on the gear faces. The ratios are very precisely machined, and are lightweight and compact to reduce inertia, thereby improving engine responsiveness. They run on highly specialised, high-efficiency bearings.

Gearchanges are undertaken extremely rapidly. Ferrari's F2002 car is believed to have a gearchange time of five-hundredths of a second — a 15% improvement on the previous year's model.

A Formula 1 gearbox makes exceptional demands on the synthetic gear oil that lubricates and cools it. Gearbox oil temperatures can reach 150 degrees C (although 130 degrees C is a more usual operating temperature), and the pressures between the gear teeth are phenomenal. It is incredible to think that, at any given time, virtually the entire motive power of the engine is being transmitted through a fingerprint-sized area of the gear tooth surface — and, theoretically at least, metal never touches metal: contact is limited to the oil film.

A dedicated radiator or heat-exchanger, mounted in a sidepod, cools the gearbox oil. A heat-exchanger differs from a radiator in using the engine cooling water to cool the gearbox oil (water and oil are held in a common matrix, though they do not physically come into contact with each other), rather than having air run through it to achieve cooling.

The next step along the drivetrain, the differential, also endures a punishing workload. Formula 1 cars have hydraulically actuated, electronically controlled differentials incorporating load sensors which constantly measure the torque generated by the driveshafts and make adjustments to the drive according to a pre-programmed regime. The driver can override this if he so wishes, to adjust the car's handling under acceleration out of corners.

Angled rearwards and upwards from the differential, the driveshafts cope with enormous forces — vicious torsional, or twisting, loads. At their extremities are 'tripod joints'. These are much smaller than the constant-velocity (CV) joints they have replaced in recent years, and they are also more efficient in the configuration in which they operate (at angles of less than 10 degrees). The driveshafts are angled rearwards to allow the gearbox to be moved further forward, improving the car's overall weight distribution.

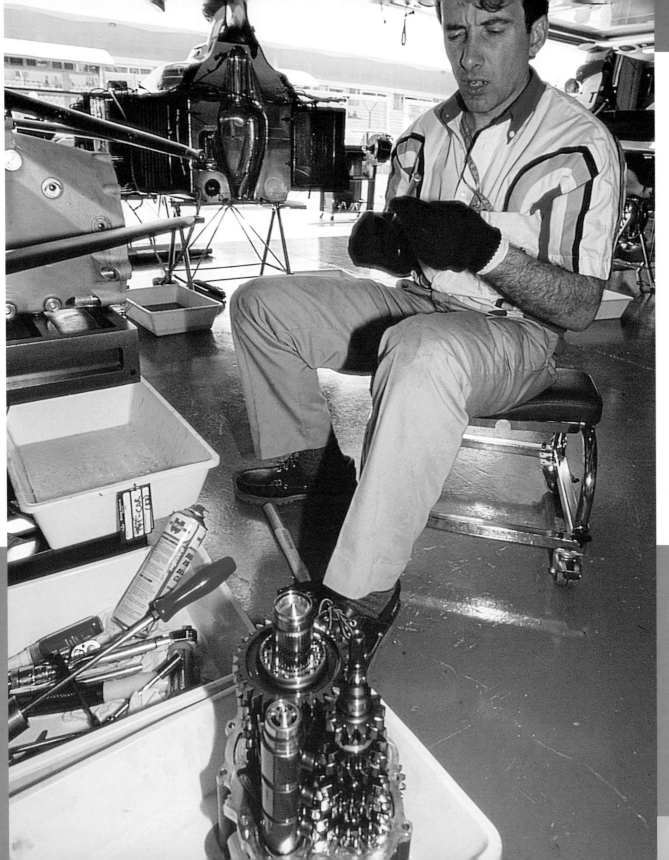

BRAKES

FORMULA 1 cars do everything quickly — even slowing down! The dazzling performance of the brakes is a 'mirror image' of the power of the engine and the grip of the tyres, reining back the enormous kinetic energy that has been unleashed. Travelling at 320 kph (200 mph) on a long straight on a dry racetrack, the top Formula 1 drivers leave themselves just 100 metres (330 feet) and three seconds to decelerate to 80 kph (50 mph) for a slow corner.

BRAKES TURN kinetic energy into heat. When the calipers grab the discs, the brakes smoulder dull red, then glow bright yellow as friction between the discs and pads generates temperatures as high as 1000 degrees C.

The brake pedal requires a deft touch — but also huge pressure: typically 150 kg (330 lb), generating well over 1000 psi in the hydraulic lines. Power-assisted braking is banned by the regulations.

Brake discs on Formula 1 cars are made of carbon-carbon (carbonfibre amalgamated with carbon). They are a far cry from the cast-iron discs they had in the past, which became less efficient the hotter they grew. By contrast, carbon-carbon discs only perform to their full potential once they have been brought up to a very high operating temperature, and they do not melt or distort.

But even carbon-carbon discs have their limitations. If they get excessively hot they start to lose their efficiency, so to help maintain them within the optimum temperature band they are perforated with cooling holes and ventilated by ram-air directed at strategic points by carbonfibre ducts. If a brake disc overheats for any reason, it fails spectacularly — centrifugal force giving the impression that its sudden disintegration is an explosion.

The diameter of Formula 1 brake discs is 28 cm (10.1 in.). This is dictated by the fact that the discs are installed within the wheels, which have a maximum permissible diameter of 33 cm (13 in.).

In its efforts to limit brake performance in the interests of safety, the FIA restricts the size and positioning of the brake ducts. The regulations also restrict the thickness of the discs to 28 mm (1.1 in.), the intention being to force brake manufacturers to limit the friction between the discs and the pads to ensure they last the race distance, thereby curbing braking performance. The logic behind this is questionable, because the real limitation is the fact that if friction between the discs and pads exceeds a certain level, the tyres will lock up under braking. The maximum deceleration achievable is about 5 G, on a dry racetrack.

Formula 1 brake pads are made from carbon-carbon, like the brake discs. The pistons are machined from titanium, as it is lightweight and very tolerant to heat. All of the cars have six-piston calipers, the maximum permitted by the regulations, on all four wheels. Brake calipers have to be very stiff and strong, otherwise they will flex under the immense strain of heavy braking, yet they must be as lightweight as possible. They are machined from a solid block of high-grade aluminium alloy.

Metal-matrix composites (MMCs) — created by mixing in materials such as silicon carbide — enable stiffer, stronger, lighter calipers to be produced, but these exotic materials were outlawed from Formula 1 caliper construction in 1998. The prohibition was introduced to limit performance and contain costs. Some idea of how costs can go through the roof when such limits are not imposed can be gained from the fact that calipers made from another exotic material — aluminium beryllium — some years ago, cost $9000 apiece!

The circuits that impose the greatest strain on the brakes are those that require lower downforce settings, because when the car has low aerodynamic drag the brakes have to do more work to slow the car down. In a high-downforce set up, on the other hand, as much as 1 G of deceleration can be generated just by the driver lifting his foot off the throttle pedal. At the end of the longest straights at Hockenheim, Montreal and Monza, the brakes have their severest test.

Two manufacturers produce Formula 1 brake units, each supplying 50 per cent of the teams at the time of writing. One is the British manufacturer AP Racing, the other is the Brembo concern of Italy. The

regulations governing Formula 1 braking systems are so prescriptive that there are only minor variations on the two designs across the full grid of cars.

For safety reasons, Formula 1 cars must have two separate brake circuits (operated by the same pedal). This ensures that if one circuit fails, the other will still act on at least two of the wheels. Although anti-lock braking systems were outlawed back in 1993, on the grounds that they diminished the degree of skill required to drive a car on the limit, drivers can adjust the braking balance between the front and rear wheels to help avoid locking one pair under heavy braking.

Typically, on a dry racetrack, around 55 per cent bias is placed on the front wheels, but when running in wet conditions a driver may transfer the braking bias slightly to the rear, because by ensuring the rear wheels lock first he can maintain control of the front wheels to prevent a spin.

FIA regulations decree that brake-balance systems must be manually operated. A sophisticated electronic/hydraulic brake-balance system — pre-programmed for each corner — was introduced by Williams in 1997, and other teams followed suit, but these systems were banned for 1998 as part of a wide-ranging purge on electronic driver aids.

Master cylinders in Formula 1 braking systems are machined from a solid block of high-grade aluminium alloy.

Even the time a driver takes to lift his foot off the accelerator pedal and locate it on the brake pedal represents vital split-seconds lost, so all Formula 1 drivers now employ left-foot braking. There are

just two foot pedals — an accelerator pedal and a brake pedal. Instead of a clutch pedal, the cars have a hand-operated clutch activation paddle on the back of the steering wheel.

Left-foot braking has been commonplace in rallying for many years, but when this technique was adopted in Formula 1 the drivers encountered some difficulties. If a driver was unfortunate enough to spin his car, with no clutch pedal to depress with his foot and his hands flailing around on the steering wheel, he found it difficult to activate the hand-operated clutch in time to prevent the engine from stalling. With time, they mastered it.

A 'brake dynamometer' can be used to improve the performance of braking systems. These have flywheels to create inertia, and allow brake operations to be simulated in the controlled environment of the brake manufacturer's premises. Parameters such as rpm, torque, temperature and brake pedal pressure can be measured with great accuracy, and refinements tested, well away from the frantic pressures of the racetrack environment.

The most important quality a driver seeks in a braking system is consistency of operation — *repeatability* — as having a consistent degree of control allows him to stay 'on the limit' throughout the braking zone, right on the point of locking up, making maximum use of the available braking power.

If the regulations permitted more innovation and ingenuity, there would be ample scope for increasing braking performance whilst maintaining the ban on anti-lock braking systems. The drawback would be that development costs would soar as teams introduced novel systems, and safety could be compromised as cars plunged ever faster into corners.

BY KEEPING his foot on the brake pedal during pit stops, the driver makes it easier for his crew to pull the wheels off their axles (and retains vital heat in the brakes into the bargain). As a wheel comes away, a thick black cloud of carbon dust billows out from the brake unit — a potential health hazard. The pit crew wear masks to protect their lungs, and goggles to shield their eyes. The 'heat sink' from the brakes also makes the wheels very hot, but the pit crew wear fire-resistant gloves and overalls.

Back once more at racing speeds, cars sometimes run into the back of other cars under braking, causing major accidents. There has been considerable debate as to whether, in the interests of safety, Formula 1 cars should be fitted with brake lights. These were tested at Silverstone during the 2001 season, but the drivers' opinions as to the benefits were divided, and a decision was taken later in the season not to adopt them. However, Ferrari used brake lights during free practice for the United States Grand Prix at Indianapolis, at the behest of the team's Technical Director — Ross Brawn — who felt that the system should not have been rejected until it was more thoroughly evaluated.

There is still a rear-facing red light for use in poor visibility, which — due to a rule-change introduced for 2002 — has increased in size. As a further safety precaution, this light flashes when the pit lane speed limiter is engaged.

SUSPENSION, WHEELS & TYRES

6

TYRES are the single most important contributor to the phenomenal performance of contemporary Formula 1 cars. Fierce competition between the two companies that supply teams with tyres — Bridgestone and Michelin — has raised performance to hitherto unimagined levels, despite the tight restrictions imposed by the FIA on the width of the tyres and on their tread design. In 1998, the sport's governing body introduced a ruling that dry-weather tyres must have grooved treads. This was a major departure, because since 1970 the cars had run on bald-treaded tyres ('slicks') in dry weather. The purpose of the ruling was to restrict tyre performance, and thereby reduce lap speeds to safer levels, by reducing the amount of rubber in contact with the racetrack — the tyre's 'footprint'.

Formula 1 tyres are of radial ply construction and are tubeless. Their width must not exceed 381 mm (15 in.), nor be less than 356 mm (14 in.) at the rear and 305 mm (12 in.) at the front. Along with the tread pattern, the constitution of the tread — the compound — plays a crucial role in determining the level of grip (adhesion) the tyre will generate, and also plays an important part in determining the tyre's wear characteristics. The four basic ingredients of the compound are rubber polymers, carbon blacks, oils and curatives.

ALTHOUGH the grip itself is generated at the 'footprints', the driver senses the level of grip through his hands and feet — and the seat of his pants!

When a car is cornering, the loading on the outside tyres increases and the loading on the inside tyres decreases as the car's weight shifts laterally. The 'weight' on a tyre due to the combined effects of the weight of the car, the aerodynamic forces and the cornering, braking and acceleration forces is known as the tyre loading. The more a tyre is loaded in a corner, the more it slips — giving rise to the characteristics of oversteer and understeer. When these two characteristics are in balance, the car is said to be neutral.

The stiffness of the tyre sidewall construction is a very important factor in the tyre's cornering performance, because this directly influences its responsiveness to the driver's steering inputs.

In common with all rear-wheel-drive vehicles, Formula 1 cars place a greater burden on the rear tyres than the front, because the front tyres only have to cope with cornering and braking forces, whereas the rear tyres must generate tractive effort as well.

Television images of pit crews changing tyres with amazing speed and precision when the cars come in to refuel spark the public imagination and highlight the fact that Formula 1 is a *team* sport. When undertaken without incident, a pit stop rarely lasts over seven seconds. Between races, the pit crew spends hours relentlessly choreographing the movements of all 22 team members assigned to the exercise, then they retire to the video room to analyse and re-analyse their technique.

LIKE THE brake pads and discs, dry-weather tyres only operate at full efficiency when they have reached their high working temperature: normally around 125 degrees C at the tread. The tyres are wrapped in electrically heated blankets to bring them closer to their optimum temperature prior to the car being driven. It takes about 90 minutes to heat a tyre fully in a blanket, but only the molecular activity that occurs when the tyre is actually 'worked' on the racetrack brings it to full effectiveness.

Formula 1 tyres are equipped with valve cores that differ from those used in roadgoing car tyres in having seals capable of withstanding the much higher temperatures generated by racing conditions. Operating pressures are lower than those of most roadgoing car tyres. Varying the tyre pressures is one of the methods used to alter the handling of the car.

The quality of the air in the tyres must be carefully controlled to minimise variables in the car's set-up. The air is processed through special equipment, linked to the compressors that inflate the tyres, which converts it into a nitrogen-rich, moisture-free gas. This ensures that each tyre retains constant inflation properties regardless of when and where it was inflated, and that pressure variations due to changes in temperature are uniform. The high temperature build-up in racing conditions can result in a pressure increase of as much as 10 psi. For this reason, the pressures are always measured and set when the tyres are at the optimum operating temperature.

When a tyre is revolving at maximum speed — around 2800 rpm — the G-forces acting on the tread are phenomenal. Inevitably, compromises must be made in the design of a racing tyre. For example, it must be as light as possible, in order to reduce what is termed unsprung weight and thereby maximise roadholding, yet it has to be strong enough to withstand the enormous forces imposed on it. It has to offer as much grip as possible, yet it must have durability and offer consistent performance.

When a fresh tyre is put on a car it is referred to as a 'sticker' tyre, because it still bears the manufacturer's distinctive adhesive identification label. When it is used for the first time and brought up to operating temperature, it has undergone one heat cycle and is then described as 'scrubbed'.

The dry-weather tyre is in a class of its own — neither a direct modification of the outlawed slick, nor an adaptation of the wet-weather tyre. Its introduction and subsequent development required a fundamentally different design philosophy. FIA regulations for dry-weather tyres specify that there must be three grooves in the front tyres and four grooves in the rear tyres — all 14 mm (0.55 in.) wide, tapering to 10 mm (0.39 in.), all 2.5 mm (0.09 in.) deep and separated by 50 mm (1.97 in.).

Each driver is allocated 40 dry-weather tyres and 28 wet-weather tyres per race meeting. Only two specifications of dry-weather tyre are allowed.

WET-WEATHER tyres can only be used when the racetrack has been officially declared 'wet' by the Race Director. Although they have a similar construction to dry-weather tyres, their tread pattern is very different.

The grooves in the tread are designed to disperse as much water as possible, allowing the tread to grip the racetrack surface. FIA regulations demand that 75 per cent of the tread area of a wet-weather tyre must be 'land', and 25 per cent 'sea' — meaning that a quarter of the total tread area must be composed of grooves.

The aim when designing a wet-weather tyre is to ensure that it will operate effectively across a wide spectrum of conditions, ranging from a damp to a partially flooded racetrack. The tyre must therefore be capable not only of removing whatever water is encountered, but also of maintaining its temperature so as to sustain optimum performance from the tyre compound. The tread pattern is crucial in this respect.

Overheating can cause a tyre to deteriorate rapidly, and wet-weather tyres are particularly susceptible to this if the track surface dries out too much. In order to prevent their wet-weather tyres from overheating, drivers often seek out a 'wet' racing line on a drying circuit by avoiding the 'tram lines' which emerge when cars have cleared standing water or moisture from the conventional racing line.

THE TWO tyre manufacturers must transport to each Grand Prix all of the equipment necessary to fit the tyres to the wheels, inflate them, balance and demount them. They also bring computer equipment with which to undertake stock control and relay technical data to the main computers at their respective headquarters for further analysis.

Tyre technicians assigned to each team by the tyre manufacturers are kept busy throughout a Grand Prix meeting. One ongoing task is to monitor the state of the tyres every time a car comes into the pits. The temperature and wear information they record provides a vital guide to the performance not only of the tyres, but also of the chassis and suspension. These data may also identify a change in the characteristics of the circuit, which may have been partially or wholly resurfaced since the last time it was visited by Formula 1 cars.

An important factor in winning races is conserving the tyres. The driver's actions, the nature of the racetrack surface, and the track surface temperature — or a combination of all three — can damage the surface of a tyre sufficiently to severely degrade its performance. Common problems are graining, which is a 'tearing' of the tread surface generally caused by excessive lateral grip, and blistering, which is caused by overheating of the tread compound. The driver can shift the braking bias on the car, for instance from the rear to the front tyres if the rear tyres blister, in order to help conserve them.

LOCKING A TYRE by applying the brakes too hard — as seen here — can also severely degrade its performance, as the resultant flat spot causes vibration. Triple world drivers' champion Niki Lauda, now chief of the Jaguar Formula 1 team, described this most expressively as 'the rape of a tyre'.

Formula 1 wheels are supplied by specialist manufacturers, such as BBS. They are made from forged magnesium. FIA regulations stipulate that all four wheels must be connected to the chassis by wire tethers, to prevent them flying off in the event of a major accident. Under a new regulation introduced for 2002, the strength of these wheel tethers was increased by 20 per cent.

Because the rear tyres have a higher workload than the front tyres, the maximum permissible rear wheel width is employed. The team and its tyre manufacturer then jointly select a width for the front wheels that will balance the rear.

Wheels look set to become the latest thing in mobile billboards. A British company, Adflash, has developed WheelFX, a device which uses light-emitting diodes (LEDs) to recreate logos that appear to be static as the wheels revolve!

To keep as much of the suspension system as possible out of the airflow, thereby reducing aerodynamic drag, the shock-absorbers — more usually called dampers — are mounted internally. At the front of the car they are mounted length-wise on top of the chassis, just in front of the cockpit aperture, covered by a streamlined hatch. At the rear of the car they are mounted on top of the gearbox casing — again, lengthwise — shrouded by the engine cover. Some cars have twin-damper systems at the front and rear, while others have triple-damper arrangements at both ends, and a few have a combination of these configurations. Many teams tailor their own dampers from proprietary components supplied by Penske, while others have dampers made for them by two specialist manufacturers, Koni and Sachs.

Loads generated by the car's interaction with the racetrack are fed to the dampers by diagonal pushrods acting via rocker assemblies on top of the chassis and gearbox. These rockers direct the forces through 90 degrees, converting the linear (push-pull) motion into rotary motion.

Not all Formula 1 cars have springs around their dampers in the conventional manner. Many have torsion bars instead of springs, often mounted directly to the rockers to offer resistance to their rotation. A torsion-bar arrangement tends to reduce friction and mass in the suspension, making it more responsive, and also allows the car's ride-height to be adjusted more rapidly.

All of the cars have an anti-roll mechanism in the front suspension, and some have an anti-roll mechanism at the rear as well. These systems operate in much the same manner as those on roadgoing vehicles, resisting the car's tendency to roll under cornering forces, but they are much lighter. Adjusting the anti-roll mechanism is the primary method of controlling understeer and oversteer. This is very much a matter of personal preference for the driver. McLaren's Kimi Räikkönen, for example, prefers a little oversteer to understeer, although he ideally likes his car to be neutral.

At the outer extremities of the four suspension assemblies, retained by upper and lower wishbones, are the uprights. These connect the pushrods to the axle/wheel-bearing assemblies and brake units (and, in the case of the front suspension, the steering arms as well), and fit neatly within the wheels to keep them out of the airflow. Almost all contemporary Formula 1 uprights are made of titanium to reduce

unsprung weight and thereby improve the car's handling, and the pushrods, wishbones and steering arms are made of carbonfibre, rather than steel which was used in the past for the same reason.

The wishbones, pushrods and steering arms are highly streamlined to reduce air resistance, but the FIA places strict limitations on the extent to which suspension elements can be used as aerodynamic aids.

One of the key differentiators between a winning car and an also-ran is the ability to tolerate the unsettling effects of riding the kerbs. Drivers will often seek to use the kerbs in their search for elusive fractions of seconds, improving their line through particular corners. Imola is an example of a circuit where use of the kerbs plays an important role in determining lap times.

The better-equipped teams test the dynamic performance of the suspension on test rigs in the relative comfort of their headquarters. The car is mounted on a complex system of hydraulics that imposes loads duplicating those fed into the car on the racetrack. The hydraulics are commanded by software downloaded from runs made by the team's other cars on specific circuits, perhaps even that same day, and captured by on-board instrumentation (the data-acquisition system). The test rigs are known as 'seven-post' rigs because there are four hydraulic actuators for the wheels — one under each wheel — and three bolted to the chassis to impose loads simulating downforce and rolling movements.

A seven-post rig can simulate, for example, the loads that are fed into the car's front and rear suspension in high-speed corners, including loads induced by bumps and undulations in the racetrack surface. Braking and acceleration loads can be fed in simultaneously, as can aerodynamic loads, either independently or simultaneously.

THE COCKPIT ENVIRONMENT

7

ASSAILED by G-forces, battered by braking, and jostled from all sides by his peers, the driver of a Formula 1 car cannot rest for a moment. His cockpit is a cocoon of safety, but it is here that he endures a rigorous and unrelenting test — both physical and mental. The physical strains on a Formula 1 driver are truly enormous. Lateral G-forces of 3.5 G can be experienced through high-speed corners — equating to a load of 30 kg (65 lb) being exerted on the driver's neck muscles.

The forces of acceleration and deceleration are no less severe. Those same neck muscles must react to almost constant fore-and-aft forces as the car plunges into corners under braking, then rapidly gathers speed again. At 2 G, the forces of acceleration are more manageable — aided by a cockpit head-rest — but braking forces are an entirely different matter. Hanging in their safety harnesses, the drivers are subjected to deceleration levels as high as 5 G at the point when the wheels lock.

High G-forces experienced during heavy braking and hard cornering can impair the driver's vision, as the flow of blood to his eyes is restricted. Peripheral vision deteriorates, and perspective is distorted. Severe bumps in the racetrack surface can be even more disorienting, the sudden vertical G-forces momentarily draining the blood from the driver's eyes. At Brazil's Interlagos — a switchback of a circuit, notorious for its bumps — some corners have to be driven virtually 'blind'.

A HUMAN heart normally functions at 60–80 beats per minute, but when a Formula 1 driver is operating at qualifying and race speeds, his heart rate can soar way beyond that. Rates of 160–190 beats per minute are not unusual in such conditions, and rates as high as 210 beats per minute have been recorded. This could be fatal to a person not totally fit.

Over a race distance, the forces acting upon the driver are extremely punishing, hence the need for peak physical fitness. His neck muscles must be highly developed to cope with the high lateral and longitudinal G-forces. His upper body, arms and hands must be muscular enough not only to deal with the vertical G imposed by bumps and undulations in the racetrack surface, but also to turn the steering wheel when the 'weight' of the car has risen under the influence of high aerodynamic downforce levels at higher speeds, making the effort of steering more strenuous. A Formula 1 car 'weighs' over a ton at 240 kph (150 mph).

To make matters worse, cockpit temperatures can soar to 50 degrees C. Swathed in multi-layer fireproof garments, the driver dehydrates and becomes fatigued — and as his stamina is sapped, his concentration starts to fade. To replenish some of the lost liquid and vitamins, he sips an energy-giving drink through a pipe fed into the front of his crash helmet. Some drivers even wear the stick-on plastic devices favoured by athletes, which open the nostrils to aid breathing.

In spite of these measures, up to a litre of body fluid — around 2 kg (4 lb) — may be lost during a two-hour race.

www.jaguar-rac

HSBC

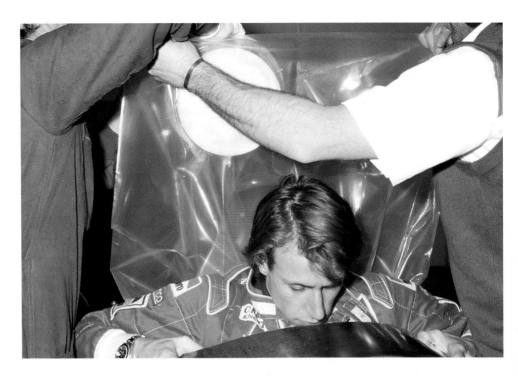

IF A DRIVER is not properly supported by his seat, he will be continually 'fighting' his car — resisting the incessant G-forces — and will not be capable of driving to his full potential. A form-fitting seat is therefore made for each driver, profiled to his own unique shape to provide the necessary support. The seat-fitting usually takes place at the team's factory (pictured during his seat-fitting is Ferrari test driver Luca Badoer).

A large plastic bag is placed in the cockpit, and the driver clambers in and sits on the bag, leaning forward and raising himself up slightly while a concoction of chemicals is poured in. The concoction is an equal mix of two chemical agents that react when mixed together immediately before being poured into the bag. The chemical reaction creates a foam-like substance that expands within the bag and then solidifies, conforming exactly to the driver's contours.

When the driver feels the foam starting to solidify, he adopts what he feels is the most comfortable position in the car and holds that position — using the bag as a seat as it begins to support him — whilst the chemical reaction goes through its final stages.

Afterwards, the plastic bag is stripped away and excess foam is trimmed from the edges of the moulding. The seat is then given several coats of resin to harden it further, ensuring that it will withstand the rigours of racetrack use. The team keeps a copy of a driver's form-fitting seat in the pit garage ready in case he has to change cars, for instance switching to the spare car after a mishap with his own during a qualifying session.

The moulded seat is mounted into a seat 'shell' that can be rapidly removed, allowing an injured driver to be lifted out of the car whilst still fully supported. This would significantly reduce the risk of permanently disabling a driver who has sustained spinal injuries.

THE CRASH helmet is a vital piece of safety equipment, and the FIA's regulations set out very specific requirements to ensure that the wearer is adequately protected. A key function of the crash helmet is protecting the driver's brain from injury in the event of an accident. The human brain is not firm and grey as generally supposed, but pink in colour (because of the blood coursing through it) and soft, with a consistency akin to thick porridge. It is so soft that it cannot even support its own weight. Within the tough, boney shell of the cranium it is protected by a cushion of cerebrospinal fluid and meninges. Nevertheless, it is susceptible to damage if subjected to the high forces experienced in a crash.

Crash helmets have evolved considerably over the years, but the fundamental design principles remain unchanged. The helmet's hard outer shell is, in effect, a secondary cranium, protecting the wearer from scull fractures in all but the worst cases, while its compressible foam lining soaks up impact forces, reducing the effects of sudden deceleration on the brain. Within Formula 1, the most popular crash helmets are made by the American manufacturer, Bell, and the Japanese company, Arai. The shell typically has an immensely strong carbon/aramidic fibre-weave construction.

Aerodynamics play a part in the design of the crash helmet. Wind tunnel testing is undertaken to refine its shape so as to provide a smooth flow of air into the airbox (engine air inlet) immediately above the driver's head. Aerodynamic refinements such as 'trip strips' and other sculpted features on the helmet also reduce its tendency to lift at high speed, and smooth out the airflow to reduce buffeting, which can upset the driver's concentration. Some cars have a vestigial windscreen, or a sliver-like carbonfibre fairing around the forward edge of the cockpit aperture, for the same purpose.

FOR COMFORT — and style! — drivers' overalls are custom-made. They are also highly functional. For example, the epaulettes are reinforced so the driver can be pulled from the cockpit if he is incapacitated in an accident. Although fire is not the hazard it once was in Formula 1, the risk is still taken very seriously. Drivers wear quadruple-layer, lightweight overalls made from a weave of flame-resistant Nomex fibres. FIA regulations stipulate that an 800-degree C liquid propane flame be blasted onto a section of fabric for 12 seconds to verify its flame-resistance. Although this test inflicts severe damage on the outermost layer, the level of protection is such that the innermost layer sustains only moderate scorching. In fact, the Nomex overalls will protect the driver for 30 seconds against direct flame penetration.

Under their overalls, drivers wear a long-sleeved roll-neck Nomex vest, and some wear 'long johns' for extra protection. The knees, elbows and ankles can receive painful knocks within the tight confines of the cockpit, so many drivers wear additional padding in these places. Their Nomex gloves have extra padding to guard their knuckles, and suede palms to prevent blisters and improve their grip on the steering wheel. For added fire-protection, the drivers wear Nomex-lined suede boots over their fireproof socks (the boots have flat soles for enhanced dexterity on the foot pedals), and a Nomex balaclava completes the head-to-toe security.

Formula 1 drivers are extremely fussy about their racewear. The high lateral G-forces experienced during cornering can impose a load on the hips equivalent to 100 kg (220 lb), so some drivers specify that certain seams on their overalls are repositioned so they do not rub and cause discomfort.

FIA inspectors examine the drivers' racewear during scrutineering to ensure that they comply with the regulations, and random spot-checks are sometimes undertaken after races.

FORMULA 1 steering wheels are masterpieces of engineering, as far removed from their conventional counterparts as the cars themselves are from their roadgoing cousins. The cost of a Formula 1 steering wheel is around $42,000, providing some indication of its sophistication. Being made of carbonfibre, it typically weighs just 1 kg (2 lb), or less. Instrument panels, *per se*, have disappeared from Formula 1 cars. There are a few switches and indicators on the forward rim of the cockpit aperture, but the steering wheel itself has effectively become the instrument panel. At the top of the steering wheel there is at least one LCD providing a wide range of information to the driver — oil pressure, fuel state, and so forth. In some conditions, steering wheel-mounted LCDs can be difficult to read.

Using a panoply of dials and buttons on the steering wheel, the driver can adjust the brake balance, fuel mixture and differential, engage traction control, 'launch control' (for race starts), the pit-lane speed-limiter, and the gearbox neutral selector, and speak to his team on the pit wall via the two-way radio link using a 'PTT' — push-to-talk — button.

Every team has its own unique steering wheel layout, and drivers also have some input into the design, so even team-mates may have subtly different layouts. Steering wheels on the Ferraris and Saubers feature a map of the racetrack, with each corner numbered so the driver and his engineer can be sure they are talking about the same corner. On Ferrari's steering wheel, six small dials control everything the driver needs to adjust (the dials have different colours, to help the driver avoid mistakes). In contrast, the Renault's steering wheel has one large central dial that the driver turns to select the desired function, then he alters the settings by pressing various buttons.

For lightness and precision, the steering column is 'gun-barrelled' from a solid bar of titanium. The high-nosed configuration of Formula 1 cars results in the steering column being virtually horizontal, so a complex set of gears and bevels is required to convert the driver's steering inputs through almost 90 degrees to the steering rack. It is important that any tendency for wear in the rack and pinion during the course of a race is minimised, as that would introduce unwelcome 'play' into the steering system. Racks have evolved considerably in recent years, becoming lighter, smaller and more efficient as a result of better design and materials. Titanium is now the standard material for Formula 1 racks.

A circuit such as Monaco is particularly hard on the driver's hands and wrists. Power-assisted steering systems — now outlawed — had offered around 30 per cent assistance, which was sufficient to ease the physical strain of driving the car without removing the all-important 'feel' from the steering. The prohibition was a move by the FIA to head off any possibility of drivers being aided in their task (or even, *theoretically*, replaced altogether) by electronic systems operated via telemetry by team personnel seated at TV monitors in the pits...

Formula 1 cockpits are so cramped that the steering wheel must be removed before the driver can climb out of his car (or be lifted out if he is incapacitated). To ensure that he will be able to climb out rapidly in an emergency, FIA regulations specify that the time required for the driver to remove the steering wheel, get out, then replace the wheel, must not exceed ten seconds. To release the steering wheel, the driver pulls back on a mechanism at the top of the steering column. The regulations specify that the driver must replace the steering wheel if he abandons his car on the racetrack, in order to speed the progress of trackside marshals tasked with recovering the car.

Contemporary Formula 1 gearboxes are usually operated in an automatic mode, particularly for upshifts, via the car's electronic control system. Some drivers prefer to use the gearbox in a semi-automatic mode, as they wish to initiate downshifts themselves as part of their braking technique, and also wish to exercise greater control on downshifts as they negotiate the pit lane for a refuelling stop. They

do so with fingertip precision using either one, or sometimes two, levers on the back of the steering wheel — one for downshifts, the other, if it is fitted, for upshifts — to activate either high-pressure hydraulics or pneumatics in the gearshift mechanism.

Close to the driver's other hand is the clutch activator. Formula 1 drivers do not need to use the clutch to change gear, nor do they use it at the start of the race, because software does that work for them. The only times a driver uses the clutch are: when he pulls out of his pit garage; at the start of the formation lap (to lay rubber down to improve his race start); when he spins the car (to prevent the engine stalling); and (in the case of some, but not all, drivers) during pit stops, to exercise greater control.

A FULLY-adjustable safety harness secures the driver firmly in his seat. There are two shoulder straps, two lap straps and two crotch straps, connected by a quick-release buckle. FIA regulations stipulate that the straps must be 75 mm (2.95 in.) wide, and the driver must be able to release the belts and climb out of the car within five seconds. Padded 'sleeves' are pulled over the shoulder straps to protect the driver's collar-bones in the event of a heavy impact.

Manufacturers of Formula 1-specification safety harnesses include Willans, based in the UK, and TRW/Sabelt, based in Italy.

In a major frontal impact, forces can be so massive that the driver's head actually strikes the steering wheel. This happened to Mika Häkkinen in an accident during the 1995 Australian Grand Prix in Adelaide, in which the Finn sustained near-fatal head injuries. The material in the safety harness belts stretches and the driver's upper body and neck elongate under the enormous strain. FIA regulations therefore demand that the steering wheel should have an impact-absorbing structure incorporated into it, or the steering column should be collapsible. A 'steering wheel impact test' is conducted to verify that there is sufficient impact-absorption.

A device known as the HANS — or Head And Neck Safety device — is expected to be made compulsory for Formula 1 drivers in time for the start of the 2003 season. This is a supporting brace, worn over the shoulders and attached to the driver's crash helmet, which protects the wearer against potentially fatal 'whiplash' injuries.

To provide additional protection for the driver's head in the event of a major accident, a 'collar' of deformable padding extends virtually right around the rim of the cockpit aperture. Strict regulations govern the dimensions and positioning of the FIA-approved padding material, which must be 75 mm (2.95 in.) thick, must extend as far forward as the steering wheel, and must be removable without the need for tools.

For a driver to perform effectively, his field of vision must be taken into account at the design stage. Purely from an aerodynamic standpoint, the lower the driver can be placed in the cockpit, out of the air-flow around the car, the better. A lower seating position also helps lower the car's overall centre of gravity, improving its handling characteristics. But if a driver is seated too low in the cockpit, his restricted vision will impair his performance. On some circuits, such as the sinuous Monaco, drivers prefer to have a slightly elevated seating position, so they can judge their lines around tight corners more accurately.

The driver's forward field of vision is important, for obvious reason, but so is his view backwards. Unless the driver has an awareness of the positions of his opponents' cars relative to his own, he cannot adequately defend his racing line. Worse, he may pose a hazard to faster cars. The size and positioning of the rear-view mirrors are therefore critical, and both size and position are governed by the regulations — being verified by FIA inspectors during scrutineering by means of a visual recognition test involving numbered boards placed behind the car. For the 2002 season, the regulations demanded a 20 per cent increase in the size of the rear-view mirrors.

Drivers are sometimes penalised for failing to respond to the warnings of trackside marshals, when flags are flown to alert them to potential dangers. Drivers thus accused frequently claim that they had not seen the signal, either because they were momentarily preoccupied or because their view of the flag was temporarily obscured by other cars. In an effort to assist drivers in such circumstances, experiments have been conducted with a system of colour-coded lights in the cockpit that could one day supplement the flag marshals' trackside signals.

ON THE racetrack, the driver can communicate with his team via a two-way VHF radio link. There is a small microphone immediately in front of the driver's mouth, and there are tiny speakers embedded in soft acrylic earpieces, moulded to the contours of his ears for maximum comfort and efficiency (the close fit shuts out external noise, such as the din from the engine). In the pits there is no need for the radio: a 'hardwire' connection is plugged in directly. Here, Jacques Villeneuve is pictured in conversation with his race engineer, Jock Clear, while in the other shot Ferrari's Ross Brawn advises his drivers, Michael Schumacher and Rubens Barrichello, on race strategy from the pit wall.

Because the key topic of conversation is race strategy, radio transmissions are scrambled to prevent eavesdropping by rival teams and the media. However, the encryption codes must be shared with the FIA to counter the possibility of infringements such as race-rigging.

THE EXPERIENCE of Formula 1 can now be enjoyed by a wider range of people, thanks to the development of passenger-carrying versions of the race cars. McLaren started the trend with its two-seater in 1998. The passenger sits behind the driver, which restricts the view directly forward, but otherwise the sensations are identical to those experienced by the driver. The Minardi team also has a tandem two-seater, but the Arrows squad has gone one better by developing a three-seat Formula 1 car. In this radically different vehicle — dubbed the Arrows AX3 — the two passengers sit slightly behind and outboard, either side of the driver's position, with the result that they can see directly forward and feel the powerful surge of the airflow full-on.

To compensate for the extra weight of their passengers, the two- and three-seat Formula 1 cars have much smaller fuel tanks. Other modifications are necessary to compensate for alterations in the cars' weight distribution — for example, subtle changes to the suspension geometry.

FOR THOSE not lucky enough to get a ride in these incredible cars, on-board digital cameras are the method by which the experience of Formula 1 racing is conveyed to the mass audience. Mesmerising views from these cameras — which are housed in streamlined fairings on the cars — have transformed the public's perception of Formula 1. Each fairing contains a transmitter and a receiver, as well as the camera itself, which occupies only a very small space. A strip of clear film spools past the lens, keeping the picture free of dead insects, oil and other accumulating debris.

The experience of driving a Formula 1 car used to be the exclusive preserve of the racers themselves, plus a few privileged journalists. But in recent years, the phenomenon of the test driver has arisen. These skilled individuals, distinguished racers in their own right, share the burden of testing and developing the cars with the lead drivers. At least two drivers have used a test-driving role as a stepping stone to a place in the race line-up: Damon Hill and David Coulthard both gained top-flight positions at Williams in this way. Since those days, the ranks of test drivers have swelled year upon year — in 2002 the BAR team has no fewer than four testers: Anthony Davidson, Ryo Fukuda, Patrick Lemarie, and Darren Manning.

Formula 1 drivers perform their feats of car control virtually unseen in the cockpit, yet their every move is being monitored — and, moreover, *recorded* for detailed analysis. Every movement of the steering wheel, throttle pedal and brake pedal, and every adjustment the driver makes to the brake balance, fuel mixture and other controllable parameters are measured by on-board sensors. So, too, are data from a myriad of other sources — for example, the individual brake temperatures and wear rates, the movements of the suspension, the engine's fuel flow rate, revs, oil temperature and oil pressure. Some of this information is stored on a data-acquisition system and downloaded once the car returns to the pits, while the most vital data are instantaneously relayed to the team by telemetry.

A key benefit of data acquisition is that teams can compare the performance of their two drivers on particular parts of the racetrack to discover how vital split-seconds are being won and lost.